THE PENGUIN MODERN
ENGLISH LANGUAGE READER

THE PENGUIN MODERN ENGLISH LANGUAGE READER

Everyday Modern English Texts With Practice Activities

Ronald Carter

PENGUIN BOOKS

PENGUIN BOOKS

Published by the Penguin Group
Penguin Books Ltd, 27 Wrights Lane, London w8 5TZ, England
Penguin Books USA Inc., 375 Hudson Street, New York, New York 10014, USA
Penguin Books Australia Ltd, Ringwood, Victoria, Australia
Penguin Books Canada Ltd, 10 Alcorn Avenue, Toronto, Ontario, Canada M4V 3B2
Penguin Books (NZ) Ltd, 182–190 Wairau Road, Auckland 10, New Zealand

Penguin Books Ltd, Registered Offices: Harmondsworth, Middlesex, England

Published by Penguin Books 1996
10 9 8 7 6 5 4 3 2 1

Set in Monophoto Bembo
Typeset by Datix International Limited, Bungay, Suffolk
Printed in England by Clays Ltd, St Ives plc

CONTENTS

INTRODUCTION

This book offers a selection of contemporary everyday English texts that speakers of English in Britain and the United States encounter in their daily lives. The texts provide reading practice, information about everyday life and culture, and language tasks designed to increase knowledge of modern English vocabulary and grammar in use.

The reading passages include technical and business English, advertisements, office memos and official documents. The texts are grouped in different categories for purposes of study. A final section compares and contrasts texts on the same subject matter.

Throughout the book, grammar and style notes point out differences in the kinds of English used. Glossaries define over 1,000 words, abbreviations and cultural terms, and all descriptions are written in the Penguin English 3,000-word syllabus. In most cases I have given a single meaning for a word in its particular context only.

The fifty units of the book can be read in any order, in class or by students working on their own. Language practice exercises are graded: Task A is a vocabulary gap-filling exercise; Task B mainly requires some re-writing of vocabulary and grammar; Task C is an open-ended writing and discussion exercise. Answers to all A and B exercises are given at the back of the book but the main aim is for learners to work out answers for themselves by reading and re-reading the texts carefully.

At the end of this book is a guide to metric equivalents of English weights and measures mentioned in some of the texts.

Persuasive and Advertising Language

1 TRAINERS FOR WOMEN

You've got heart. You've got drive.
REEBOK BELIEVES in the athlete IN ALL OF US.

AZTREK: Running is your life. Here's your life support. The
Reebok Aztrek. A rugged running shoe with a medially
posted dual density midsole and Hexalite lightweight cushioning. Life is so hard. So is asphalt. One of them just got
easier. Maybe two.

SATELLITE: You play, you lift, you train, you run. And you
wear the Reebok Satellite, a lightweight cross training shoe
with a running profile and Hexalite to cushion the heel,
because it's a truly runnable cross trainer. And you keep on
running.

AEROSTEP PRO: You never compromise. You wear the
Reebok Aerostep Pro. With its Graphlite arch, there's no
compromising weight for support. So it's perfect for Step
Reebok class or any aerobics class. In fact, it might even be
the most versatile shoe in its class.

TELOS: What you've got in your head is a whole planet full
of mountains, trails, challenges. So what you need on your
feet is a serious hiking shoe made from a whole bunch of
recycled and environmentally sensitive materials. The
Reebok Telos. How close to the earth do you want to get?

REEBOK
For more information about Reebok products for women, call 1–800–843–4444

(Advertisement for Reebok International, 1994)

GLOSSARY

trainers (heading) special shoes that people wear for running or jogging

life support (line 3) the things that human beings need to survive

rugged (line 4) tough and strong

dual density (line 5) density is another word for thickness; dual means 'twice' or 'double'

Hexalite/Graphlite (lines 5, 14) types of rubber

cushioning (line 6) materials which make the sole of the shoe soft and comfortable like a cushion

asphalt (line 6) a hard surface used for making roads

profile (line 10) a main feature. Here, a shoe which is mainly used for running or jogging

compromise (line 13) to agree to do or to be something which is not entirely what you want

there's no compromising weight for support (lines 14–15) the shoes are not made heavier to give you support

aerobics (line 16) a form of exercise which strengthens your heart and lungs

versatile (line 17) used for many different purposes

trail (line 19) a path, usually across land which is difficult to cross

challenge (line 19) to do something difficult because you want to

hiking (line 20) a sport in which you walk long distances across difficult ground

recycled (line 21) materials which are used again

environmentally sensitive (line 21) materials which do not damage the world around us when they are used

GRAMMAR AND STYLE NOTES

1   When you put other nouns in front of the main noun in English, then this is one way in which a scientific and technical style is created. 'Dual density midsole'/ 'Hexalite . . . cushioning' suggest that the trainer has been scientifically designed.

2   The writers of this advertisement use words which make it sound as if they are speaking to you directly. The personal pronouns 'you' and 'your', direct questions (line 22) and informal conjunctions such as 'so' are used.

LANGUAGE PRACTICE

A Put in the missing words. You can find all the words in the text. The first letters of the missing words are given.

1 Good running shoes c____ the heel and have to be ver____ and r____.
2 Another word for running shoe is t____.
3 An aer____ class helps you to strengthen your heart and lungs.
4 To get everything they want top athletes should enjoy a ch____ and never com____.
5 Good running shoes can also be used for h____.
6 When something is used again, it is r____.

B Substitute the underlined words with a word or words from the text. Make any grammatical changes which are necessary.

1 What you need on your feet is <u>a shoe which will really help you to walk long distances across difficult ground</u>.
2 Running is his life. It is <u>what he needs to keep him alive</u>.
3 Never <u>give in to something which is too easy and which you do not really want</u>.
4 Before athletes are ready for competition, they normally have to <u>prepare by running, jogging and hiking</u>.

C 1 The following words have all got more than one meaning. Look up each one in a dictionary and list the different meanings: **heart; drive; class; hard**.
2 In one sentence say why the advertisement begins: 'You've got heart'.

4

2 AMERICAN JEEP

IN THESE PARTS, you need a car that'll keep you on the road as well as take you off it. Which is why the locals drive a Jeep Cherokee.

Its full time or part time four-wheel drive gives unrivalled traction on slippery surfaces.

THERE'S ALSO ABS so you can brake and steer out of trouble at the same time. (On roads like these it's nice to know you can stop when you want to.)

Instead of the usual soggy 4×4 handling, the Cherokee is taut and responsive. Not only does this make it safer to drive, it also makes it more exciting to drive.

AS DOES THE 4 litre engine under the bonnet.

And should you decide to venture further afield, you'll find the Cherokee is equally at home cruising down the freeway as it is when it's up to its axles in mud.

Mind you, being off the beaten track doesn't mean you have to rough it. THE JEEP CHEROKEE pampers you with the kind of creature comforts normally found on far more expensive cars. (Like the power adjustable front seats for example.)

Not to mention side impact protection guards and the three year warranty, which are simply comforting. AND, OF COURSE, there's that warm, secure feeling you get from being above all the other traffic. Or several hundred feet above a ravine.

JEEP
The American Legend

(Advertisement for Jeep Cherokee)

5

GLOSSARY

Jeep (heading) a small, four-wheeled vehicle that can travel over rough ground

the locals (line 2) the people who live in a particular part of a county or region or town

four-wheel drive (line 4) a vehicle in which the engine drives all four wheels, rather than only two

unrivalled (line 5) it has no rival; it cannot be beaten or bettered

traction (line 5) the car has tyres that grip the road

ABS (line 6) anti-lock braking system (abbreviation)

steer (line 6) to move the car in different directions using the steering wheel

soggy (line 9) something which is soft and wet; for example, grass becomes soggy when it rains a lot. 'Soggy handling' means that the car does not always go exactly where you want it to go

taut and responsive (line 10) the car responds well when you move the steering wheel

venture further afield (line 13) to go to places which are less easy to reach

cruising (line 14) to travel in an easy and relaxed manner

freeway (line 15) a road with several lanes and controlled places where people can join it. In British English the word 'motor-way' is used

axle[s] (line 15) a part of the car which links the wheels together

mind you (line 16) a more formal phrase, with a similar meaning, is 'on the other hand'

beaten track (line 16) a route that is used regularly

rough it (line 17) to be uncomfortable

pamper (line 17) to look after someone very well

creature comforts (line 18) things such as good food, nice clothes that make life comfortable

side impact protection guards (line 21) bars which protect the car if it is hit on the side by another car or in an accident

secure feeling (line 23) a feeling of safety

ravine (line 25) a deep valley, usually between mountains

GRAMMAR AND STYLE NOTES

1   *Technical language* See note for text 1. In this text we have 'anti-lock braking system' (ABS); 'four-wheel drive'; 'side impact protection guards'; 'power adjustable front seats'.

2   *Personal style* Note the use of the personal pronoun 'you'.
3   *Informal style* There are several examples:
   – contractions: for example, 'that'll' for 'that will'; 'it's' for 'it is'
   – informal linking words: for example, 'mind you'; 'of course'
   – sentences without main verbs: for example, 'Or several hundred feet above a ravine (lines 24–25) and subordinate clauses without main clauses, 'Which is why the locals drive a Jeep Cherokee'.

LANGUAGE PRACTICE

A   Put in the missing words. You can find all the words in the text. The first letters of the missing words are given.

1   When it is slippery, cars should have good t____.
2   When you sit above all the other traffic you feel safe and sec____.
3   ABS means you can b____ safely.
4   This car is very comfortable. Even when you run off the road you never have to r____ it.
5   In this car you simply cr____ along the roads.
6   The engine doesn't drive just two wheels; this car has f____ – w____ drive.

B   Substitute the underlined words with a word or words from the text. Make any grammatical changes which are necessary.

1   The people who live in these parts need to drive both on the road and off it.
2   This car gives you all the good things which make life comfortable.
3   The features are normally found on cars which cost far more.
4   Should you decide to go to other places which are more difficult to reach, then this is the right car for you.

C   1   A jeep is used for journeys on and off main roads. List *six* words from the advertisement which show that this jeep is for use off road.

      2   Why is the jeep 'above all the other traffic' (line 24) Answer in one sentence.

---

3   US ARMED FORCES AD

1 IN FOUR YEARS, YOU WON'T RECOGNIZE YOURSELF.

Kiesha Johnson
Hawaii/Japan teacher computer operations career counselor
5 *cash for college*

The woman you see in the mirror four years from now depends a lot on what the girl reading this ad does today. This year, over 23,000 ambitious young women, like Kiesha Johnson, will find the encouragement, opportuni-
10 ties, training and experience they need in the U.S. Armed Forces.

    Smart move. Because the military is opening more jobs to women, in more fields than ever before. Now you may be eligible for one of the new positions in aviation, or
15 serve at sea aboard a carrier or cruiser.

    Over 50,000 new jobs have opened to women in the last year alone. Every one offers you training and travel benefits, career skills and education opportunities – includ-ing the Montgomery G.I. Bill, which can help you put
20 aside over $14,000 for college, up to $30,000 in select career areas.

    In the next four years Kiesha Johnson will serve her country in Hawaii and Japan, discovering her talent for teaching and helping others. What will you be doing?

With over 200 job specialties to choose from, chances are the Armed Forces can help you get where you want to go.

See your local recruiter, or call 1-800-893-LEAD for more information. Take a look at all you can do for yourself and your country. And get a glimpse of yourself four years from now. You'll like what you see.

Make It Happen.
U.S. ARMED FORCES
Army Navy Air Force Marines Coast Guard

(Advertisement for US Armed Forces, 1995)

GLOSSARY

ad (heading) advertisement (abbreviation)

career counselor (line 4) a person who gives advice to others about jobs. In British English 'counselor' is spelled 'counsellor'

smart move (line 12) a good thing to do. A formal alternative would be 'It is a smart move'

fields (line 13) types of work

aviation (line 14) the air force, flying

carrier (line 15) a warship with a long, flat deck where aircraft can take off and land

cruiser (line 15) a large, fast warship

GI (line 19) a soldier in the United States Army

put aside (lines 19–20) to save, usually money

job specialties (line 25) different jobs which require different skills. 'Specialty' in British English is 'speciality'

recruiter (line 28) someone who gives information to people so that they will join a group or club

glimpse (line 30) to see something for a very short time

marines (line 34) people who are employed in a nation's navy

coast guard (line 34) a group in the navy which is responsible for guarding the waters near to the coast and around ports

LANGUAGE PRACTICE

A   Put in the missing words. You can find all the words in the text. The first letters of the missing words are given.

1   People who want to succeed in the jobs are am____.
2   The military is opening jobs to women in lots of different f____.
3   If you are qualified, you may be el____ for the position.
4   All of us would like to get a g____ of the future.
5   New careers can give you new sk____.
6   People can discover a t____ for teaching and helping others.

B   Substitute the underlined words with a word or words from the text. Make any grammatical changes which are necessary.

1   In four years you will look and be a different person.
2   Joining the US Armed Forces is a good and intelligent thing to do.
3   Joining the US Armed Forces can help you save over $14,000.
4   There are over 200 different types of job to choose from.

C   1   Why is the pronoun 'you' used frequently in this advertisement?
2   What is the effect of the question 'What will you be doing? (line 24) Answer in one sentence.

---

4   MOBILE PHONES AD

CHECK OUT THESE LATEST FEATURES NOW
BUILT-INTO MANY MOBILE PHONES

Much more than just a phone, many of today's

mobiles offer an unprecedented range of features designed to keep you better informed, plus added security, yet so easy to use. Just ask our expert staff for a demonstration.

CALL WAITING Lets you know when another caller is trying to contact you by the use of a discreet bleep tone.

PHONE DISPLAY Displays telephone number dialled, Signal Strength, Call Timer, Battery Strength.

ALPHA NUMBER MEMORY Enables you to associate numbers with names – so that you can retrieve telephone numbers from the memory by inputting the name of the person you wish to call.

PIN NUMBER (Personal Identification Number). Secret code to stop unauthorised users making calls from your phone.

PHONE BOOK Store your most frequently used numbers for speed dialling at the touch of a button.

CALL TIMER Shows the duration of the call so that you can keep track of costs.

CALL BARRING Allows you to bar selected numbers e.g. international calls.

CALL DIVERT Re-direct calls made to your mobile to any other number of your choice.

ANSWERING SERVICE Integral answering service records messages when you can't or don't want to answer your calls. As easy as using an ordinary answering machine.

(Advertisement for Dixon's Stores Group, UK, 1995)

GLOSSARY

mobile phone (heading) a telephone you carry around with you, powered by a battery

check out (line 1) to look at something carefully (informal)

unprecedented (line 4) something that has never happened before. Here, the size and extent of the 'range'

discreet (line 9) so quiet it can hardly be noticed

bleep (line 9) a short high-pitched sound usually made by an electrical device

associate (line 12) to link or to put together

retrieve (line 13) to search for and find

input (line 14) to type numbers or letters into a machine

unauthorized (line 17) done secretly and without permission

store (line 18) to keep something until you need it

duration (line 20) how long something lasts

keep track of (line 21) to pay attention to something so that you know where it is or what is happening

call barring (line 22) to prevent certain numbers (calls) from being dialled

divert (line 24) to change the direction of something

integral (line 26) something which is built in and fitted inside something else

GRAMMAR AND STYLE NOTE

In this ad an informal style is created by ellipsis. Ellipsis occurs when words are left out: for example, 'Secret code to stop . . .' (line 16) for '*There is* a secret code . . .'; 'As easy as using . . .' for '*It is* as easy as using . . .'

LANGUAGE PRACTICE

A The following text is an extract from a letter in which you are writing to a friend about a new mobile phone which you have bought. Your friend does not understand the new technical words and you have to explain them. Complete the letter by putting in the missing words. Most of the words are in the text and the first letters of the missing words are usually given.

I now have a new Mobile phone. It's got a wide r____ of features. For example, there is c____ w____ which lets you know when another caller is trying to c____ you. I have a special ____ number which means that no one except me can make calls without my p____. The mobile has a call timer which shows the dur____ of the call so that I know how much each call c____. It also has an answering service which re____ messages just like an ordinary telephone a____ m____.

B Answer the following questions. The answers to the questions all contain a technical word or phrase. All the words appear in the text.

  1 In call waiting how do you know another caller is trying to contact you?
  2 What is the phrase used when you wish to prevent selected numbers from being dialled?
  3 Name two things which are displayed in the phone display.
  4 What is another word for re-directing calls to another telephone number?

C Write a short paragraph (about 50 words) in which you list the main advantages and disadvantages of mobile phones.

5 SMALL ADS: LAKE DISTRICT

ABSOLUTELY best value breaks, + exciting Xmas and NY holidays. The critics choice for service, quality and elegance. See the beautiful Lake District in style. Rothay Garth Hotel Ambleside. Freephone 0500 657865

AMBLESIDE. Quality Hotel in tranquil setting with

fabulous lake views. Superb restaurant. All rooms ensuite & includes free use of private pool & superb leisure facilities. Bed & breakfast from £39.50 or DB&B £49.50 pp/pn 2 people sharing. The Waterhead Hotel 0524 585145

10 AUTUMN/WINTER BREAKS. Luxury Cottages, riverside setting fully equipped. Heated indoor pool & sauna. High Tourist Board rating. Call 0609 773791 for brochure.

BASSENTHWAITE. Exquisite ctry hse in own grounds. Ensuite/4 posters/teamkrs/CTV. DB&B Fr £44 pp pn.
15 Overwater Hall 07687 76566

BOOT Eskdale. Award winning character cottage in Lakeland's finest valley. 09467 23100

BROADOAKS. Troutbeck, W'mere 2 mls. Luxury country house in peaceful surroundings, delicious food and
20 wines, cosy log fires, 4 poster Victorian, spa and jacuzzi ensuite. Free use leisure centre. RAC highly recommended. It's simply nicer. 05394 45566

CUMBRIAN COTTAGES, 160 Lux cotts. Superb locs. Short breaks avail. 0228 662284

25 DELIGHTFUL Country House Hotel, log fires, oak beams. Lake 10 mins. All ensuite. DB&B fr £59.50 pp/pn 2 people sharing – min 2 nts. Free use of superb leisure facilities. The Wild Boar Hotel 0524 585135

30 DELIGHTFUL 2 house barn conversion slps 6/10. Ideal families. 0253 736438

EDEN VALLEY 2 lge lux. cotts. in country hse. grds. Slps 4/6 or 10 C/Brochure 01768 361 183

HEART of the Lakes. Selected cotts in central Lakeland. ETB insp & graded. 05394 32321 35

HILLTHWAITE House Windermere Thornbarrow Road, overlooking lake. All rooms ensuite (some with Jacuzzi baths). Satellite TV, teamaking, sauna. Tylo steam room and heated indoor pool solely for our guests' use. 2 nights, 5 course Dinner B&B incl. VAT only £99, 3 nights only £130. Brochure: 06394 43636 40

LAKE WINDERMERE

Christmas & New Year at Lakeside Hotel
'We overlook nothing but the Lake'

Unique 4 bedroom lodge set in its own grounds
with private lake frontage & jetty.
Breathtaking views, available for self catering all year round. 45

Brochures Tel: (05395) 31207

IT'S NOT THE CHEAPEST, simply the best! Langdale self catering lodges and apartments are now graded ETB Five Keys up to deluxe (the highest grade possible). With a few weeks available until end September at up to £150 per week off the normal rental of £590–935. Sleeps 4–8 people. Superb kitchens, bedrooms and bathrooms, lavish furnishing and equipment. Use of the Country Club pool is free – so are the exercise rooms, saunas and Langdale's own nature trail. There's also squash, tennis and a luxurious Health & Beauty salon. For further details call Paula on 015394 37302. The Langdale Estate, Great Langdale, Nr Ambleside. 50 55

(Small ads in *The Sunday Times*, August 1994)

GLOSSARY

Xmas and NY (line 1–2) Christmas and New Year

in style (line 3) in an impressive and memorable way

ensuite (line 6) a bedroom with a private bathroom

DB&B (line 8) dinner, bed and breakfast

pp/pn (line 8) per person, per night

rating (line 12) a score which is based on the quality of something

ctry hse (line 13) country house

four-poster/4-poster (line 14) a large old-fashioned bed with a tall post at each corner

teamkrs (line 14) teamakers. It is possible to make tea (and coffee) in the rooms

CTV (line 14) colour television

fr (line 14) from

character cottage (line 16) a traditionally styled, small country house

W'mere (line 18) Windermere, a lake in the Lake District

mls (line 18) miles

spa (line 20) a place where water with minerals in it bubbles out of the ground

jacuzzi (line 20) a large circular bath in which the water moves around so that you can exercise your body

RAC (line 21) Royal Automobile Club

lux cotts (line 23) luxury cottages

locs (line 23) locations, another word for places

avail (line 24) available

mins (line 26) minutes

min (line 27) minimum

nts (line 27) nights

barn conversion (line 30) a farm building made into living accommodation

slps (line 30) sleeps

ideal families (lines 30–31) ideal for families

lge (line 32) large

grds (line 32) grounds

c/brochure (line 33) colour brochure. A brochure is a booklet with pictures which gives you information

ETB (line 35) English Tourist Board ('insp': inspected by the Board)

satellite TV (line 38) television programmes transmitted by a satellite in the sky

frontage (line 46) the area which is situated at the front of the hotel

jetty (line 46) a place where a boat can be kept safely and conveniently

breathtaking (line 47) something so beautiful that it stops you from breathing for a moment

self catering (line 47) cooking and looking after yourself

nature trail (lines 56–57) a path through attractive countryside

nr (line 59) near

GRAMMAR AND STYLE NOTE

There are many abbreviations in this text. It is common in small advertisements for abbreviations to be used as they use fewer letters and thus make the ad cheaper. In this example the hotels and guest houses would need to pay the newspaper for the space to place the ad.

LANGUAGE PRACTICE

A Write out the following sentences using as many *abbreviations* as possible. All the abbreviations are in the text.

  1 There are attractive cottages for Christmas and New Year which are ideal for families.
  2 There are large, luxury rooms with teamakers.
  3 The cottages have superb locations. They sleep between six and ten people. Two miles from Ambleside.
  4 The costs are from £15 per person per night. There is a minimum stay of two nights.
  5 The rooms have colour television.
  6 Dinner, bed and breakfast costs from £50 per person.

B Put in the missing words. You can find all the words in the text. The first letters of the missing words are given.

  1 The furniture and equipment are lav____.
  2 The location for the hotel is tra____.
  3 The colour br____ will give you all the information you need.

4   In this hotel you can enjoy your holiday in el___ and in st___.

C   Write a small ad (about 50 words) which advertises three hotels or other types of similar accommodation in your own region. Make your region as attractive as possible to people who may visit the area. Use abbreviations where appropriate.

---

6   ACADEMIC BOOK CATALOGUE

1   LINGUISTICS from Polity Press

THE ART OF CONVERSATION
Peter Burke

The Art of Conversation is a major contribution to the social history of language – a relatively new field which has become the focus of lively interdisciplinary debate in recent years.

Drawing on the work of sociolinguists and others, Burke uses their concepts while reserving the right to qualify their theories where the historical record makes this seem appropriate. Like the sociolinguists, Burke is concerned with the way language varies according to who is communicating to whom, on what occasion, in what medium and on what topic. Unlike many sociolinguists, Burke adds an historical dimension, treating language as an inseparable part of social history. Among the topics discussed are the changing role of Latin; language and identity in Italy; the art of conversation; and silence, viewed as an act of communication.

Peter Burke is Reader in Cultural History at the University of 20
Cambridge and Fellow of Emmanuel College, Cambridge.

229 × 152 mm 200 pages
0–7456–1110–9 hardback c.£35.00
0–7456–1288–1 paperback c.£11.95
August 1991

25

(from Polity Press Book Catalogue, 1991)

GLOSSARY

catalogue (heading) a book containing a list of things you can
  buy (here academic books)

relatively (line 5) to quite a large extent

focus (line 6) something which has special attention

interdisciplinary (line 6) more than one subject

sociolinguist (line 8) someone who studies language in society

concept (line 9) an idea

qualify (line 10) to add something or alter it in order to improve
  it

varies (line 12) changes or alters

medium (line 14) a way of expressing something; for example, in
  speech or writing

dimension (line 15) an aspect or view

inseparable (line 16) something that cannot be broken or parted

identity (line 17) the essential features of a person or place or
  object

reader (line 20) a University lecturer of the highest grade below
  Professor

fellow (line 21) a senior member of a college, normally an Oxford
  or Cambridge University college

229 × 152 mm (line 22) the size of the book

0–7456–1110–9 (line 23) the ISBN number by which the book is
  identified

hardback (line 23) a stiff, hard cover for a book

paperback (line 24) a soft cover for a book

c £11.95 (line 24) c = circa: approximately

August 1991 (line 25) the date when this book was first published

LANGUAGE PRACTICE

A Put in the missing words. You can find all the words in the text. The first letters of the missing words are given.

   1 Soc____ is the study of language and society.
   2 Language is an in____ part of social history.
   3 Language v____ according to who is communicating to whom.
   4 Look in the cat____ to see if you can find the book which you want.
   5 You can buy the book as a h____ or as a paper____
   6 Dr Jones is a r____ in geography at the university.

B Substitute the underlined words with a word or words from the text. Make any grammatical changes which are necessary.

   1 The social history of language is <u>to a considerable extent a new field</u>.
   2 The hardback book will cost <u>approximately</u> £25.
   3 One of the main <u>subjects</u> of the book is the changing role of Latin.
   4 Silence can be <u>seen as a way to communicate</u>.

C Find a book and write a description of it using the last four lines as a model. Put in details of size, price, date etc.

---

7 INSURANCE AD

1 When you arrange home insurance with *The* Insurance Service, you pay for just the protection you want. We won't insist on one blanket level of cover or try and sell you more insurance than you really need.

5 VALUABLE DISCOUNTS We offer a No Claims Bonus that could help reduce your home insurance premiums even further!

You qualify for a discount if you have a claim-free record when you join *The* Insurance Service, and after 5 years claim-free, you could be entitled to a generous 25% discount! $\scriptstyle 10$

There are discounts available for the security-conscious, too, or if you have more than one policy with us. Just ask for details when you call for your free quotation.

A BETTER CLAIMS SERVICE You'll deal with a sympa- $\scriptstyle 15$ thetic and expert claims specialist, direct by phone, on our Claims Action Line if you are ever unlucky enough to have to make a claim on your policy.

A MONEY-BACK GUARANTEE We even offer a full 14 day money-back guarantee on all our policies, for real $\scriptstyle 20$ peace of mind (provided, of course, that you haven't made a claim).

(Advertisement for The Insurance Service, 1994)

GLOSSARY

protection (line 2) to keep someone or something safe
blanket level of cover (line 3) insurance which covers everything
no claims bonus (line 5) when no claims have been made against
 a policy, the price of the insurance is normally reduced
premium (line 6) the sum of money paid for insurance each year
discount (line 8) to reduce the price of something
claim (line 8) when you apply to the insurance company to pay
 you money
entitled (line 10) the right to have something
security-conscious (line 12) to try to protect everything yourself
quotation (line 14) the price which the insurance company say
 they will charge
claims action line (line 17) a special telephone number which you
 can ring if you have a claim
14 day money-back guarantee (line 20) a promise that you will get
 your money back if within 14 days you are not satisfied

LANGUAGE PRACTICE

A Put in the missing words. You can find all the words in the text. The first letters of the missing words are given.

1 Our company offers a n____ cl____ b____.
2 If you and your family are security-conscious, we give dis____.
3 Call us now for a free q____.
4 Insurance gives everyone pro____ and p____ of m____.
5 If you are not satisfied within 14 days, we g____ to give you your money back.
6 Our s____ is good. We even provide a special telephone number to ring if you wish to make a cl____.

B Substitute the underlined words with a word or words from the text. Make any grammatical changes which are necessary.

1 The insurance company will give a reduction on the price of the insurance on your home.
2 We guarantee to give you your money back.
3 The prices of our policies are very low.
4 You could have the right to a large discount.

C Discuss these questions with a partner who has read the text.

1 How would you feel if your house was badly damaged and you had no insurance?
2 Why is this company called *The* Insurance Service? Why is it not called *An* Insurance Service?

8   FRIENDS OF THE EARTH RECRUITMENT LEAFLET

FRIENDS OF THE EARTH
WHAT YOUR SUPPORT CAN DO

Friends of the Earth's campaigns get results – thanks to our many supporters and the weight of public opinion. By joining us you make your voice heard and help us to continue working towards:

Stopping the destruction of **tropical rainforests**
Halting **global warming**
Protecting the **ozone layer**
Preventing **air pollution** and **acid rain**
Promoting **recycling**
Forcing the clean-up **of rivers** and **drinking water**
Stopping **hazardous waste** dumping
Controlling dangerous **chemicals**, including **pesticides**
Encouraging sustainable **agriculture**
Ensuring the protection of **wildlife habitats**
Bringing about a sane and sensible **transport** policy
Seeing the phase-out of **nuclear power** in the UK
Promoting **energy efficiency** and **renewable energy**

Friends of the Earth must ensure that this is the decade of urgent environmental action. Right now, each one of us *can* make a difference. The Earth needs all the Friends it can get.

(Friends of the Earth recruitment leaflet, 1994)

GLOSSARY

campaign (line 3) here, activities which people carry out in order
　　to change things socially and politically

the weight of public opinion (line 4) a large number of people who think the same about something

tropical (line 7) the hottest parts of the world

global warming (line 8) the warming-up of the Earth's climate, due to too much carbon dioxide in the atmosphere

ozone layer (line 9) a layer of the atmosphere which protects us from some of the harmful rays of the sun

pollution (line 10) making water, air and the world around us dirty and dangerous to live in

acid rain (line 10) rain which contains a lot of acid, caused by waste gases from industry

hazardous (line 13) dangerous

dumping (line 13) throwing away

pesticide (line 14) chemicals used by farmers to kill harmful creatures, especially insects

sustainable (line 15) something we can keep doing easily and safely

wildlife habitats (line 16) the natural homes of different kinds of plants and animals

sane (line 17) based on good sense

phase-out (line 18) gradually stop using something

nuclear power (line 18) power and energy which is produced by splitting atoms

efficiency (line 19) doing a job well without wasting time or energy

renewable energy (line 19) sources of power that are there all the time, for example the sun and wave-power

urgent (line 21) something that needs to be done at once

environmental (line 21) the environment is the natural world surrounding towns and cities

GRAMMAR AND STYLE NOTES

1 Note how the final paragraph (line 20) uses modal verbs to persuade readers to act ('must', 'can').

2 The simple present tense also carries a modal force (see lines 3–6 and 20–23.) The present tense stresses that you have a lasting effect for example, 'you *make* your voice heard and *help* us . . .' The simple present tense in English often suggests something that is permanent and always true (for example, oil *floats* on water).

LANGUAGE PRACTICE

A Put in the missing words. You can find all the words in the text. The first letters of the missing words are given.

  1 Join us in our c____ to save the earth.
  2 Pollution can be very haz____.
  3 It is important to protect all wildlife in their natural h____.
  4 Tr____ rainforests are being destroyed all over the world.
  5 This is the decade of u____ action to protect the en____.
  6 We must be more ef____ in our use of energy.

B Answer the following questions. The answers to the questions all contain a technical word or phrase. All the words appear in the text.

  1 What is the phrase used to describe the fact that the world is getting warmer and warmer?
  2 What is the phrase used to describe rain which is polluted?
  3 What is the layer of the atmosphere which protects us from the sun but which is becoming dangerously thin?
  4 What is the word for the chemicals which are used by farmers to kill the pests which destroy their crops?

C From the tasks listed by Friends of the Earth choose one which you believe to be the *most* important for the environment. Write a short paragraph (about 50 words) in which you give reasons why you believe this task to be the most important.

9 USA HOLIDAYS

WASHINGTON United States

Washington is a superb City break destination and you will be pleasantly surprised to find wide boulevards, grand monuments, plenty of green open spaces and no skyscrapers!

The Mall which links Capitol Hill to the Lincoln Memorial consists of over a mile of grassy park, along which you will find some of the country's best museums – the National Air and Space Museum is particularly impressive.

The Capitol Building is worth a visit and you can walk through the historic corridors and view some of the changes.

In the evening take the metro to Union Station, one of the city's newer attractions for dinner and shopping, or to historic Georgetown, where the charming cobbled streets and the Federal period townhouses mingle with quaint restaurants, speciality shops and nightclubs.

WHAT'S INCLUDED
Return British Airways Scheduled Flights
Transfer on arrival only to your chosen hotel
Accommodation only at your chosen hotel
Services of a British Airways Holiday Representative
City Breaks travel pack including documentation, itinerary and guidebook

YOUR WASHINGTON HOTELS
1. *Savoy Suites Hotel* 3★ This modern hotel is situated near Georgetown and the National Cathedral, 15 minutes on the underground from the White House. The hotel has a shuttle bus which runs to the nearest metro station. Accommodation is in air-conditioned suites with private bath and WC, telephone, radio and TV. Other facilities include a lounge bar and restaurant.

2. *Willard Inter-continental 5★DL*   The elegant deluxe hotel is superbly located just two blocks from the White House and within easy walking distance of the Washington monument. Accommodation is in air-conditioned rooms with private bath, shower and WC, telephone, TV, radio and minibar. Other facilities include 2 lounges, a bar, shopping arcade, 2 restaurants and a health club. 35

(from a British Airways holidays brochure, 1994)

GLOSSARY

city breaks (line 2) a short holiday in a city
destination (line 2) the place to which you are going
boulevard (line 3) a very wide street
skyscraper (line 4) a very tall building
memorial (line 6) another word for monument
metro (line 11) the underground railway system in some cities
cobbled (line 13) the surface of a road which is covered with stones
Federal period (line 14) the period before American Independence
    from Britain in 1776
mingle (line 14) to join in with
quaint (line 14) attractive because it is rather unusual and old-
    fashioned
speciality shop (line 15) one which concentrates on selling particular
    things
scheduled (line 17) according to the normal timetable of the
    airline
transfer (line 18) transport from one place to another
documentation (line 21) papers
itinerary (line 21) plan of a route showing places to visit, and the
    times
shuttle bus (line 27) a bus which makes frequent journeys only
    between two places
suite (line 28) a set of rooms
deluxe hotel (line 31) an expensive hotel, luxuriously equipped
block (line 32) an area of land in a city with buildings on it and
    flats all around it

the White House (line 32) the home and offices in Washington
of the President of the United States

minibar (line 36) a selection of small bottles of mainly alcoholic
drinks, provided by the hotel

LANGUAGE PRACTICE

A Put in the missing words. You can find all the words in the
text. The first letters of the missing words are given.

1 Singapore is a wonderful holiday d____.
2 In the old town there are some charming c____ streets,
his____ buildings and q____ restaurants.
3 This is a normal sc____ flight not a special holiday
charter flight.
4 All the rooms in the hotel are a____ -c____.
5 In Washington there are wonderful wide b____ and
no sk____.
6 The hotel is superbly loc____. It is a very el____ hotel.

B Substitute the underlined words with a word or words
from the text. Make any grammatical changes which are
necessary.

1 The Capitol Building is worth seeing.
2 In Georgetown you can see townhouses together with
quaint restaurants.
3 The National Air and Space Museum creates a special
impression.
4 The hotel has a very good position just two blocks
from the White House.

C Write one paragraph (about 50 words) in which you describe the main attractions of a city you would recommend
others to visit.

Mr. Eric Forth (Mid-Worcestershire): Will my Hon. Friend concede that my right Hon. Friend the Prime Minister has two unique contributions to make to the debate? One is her considerable length of service in the House, and the comparison that she can make on that basis; but more important is her experience at the Dispatch Box during Prime Minister's Questions, about which she can express a concern that probably cannot be felt by any other Hon. Member?

Mr. Nelson: I do not concede: I thoroughly agree with my Hon. Friend. My right Hon. Friend the Prime Minister has everything to gain and little to lose from the televising of Parliament. I am constantly impressed by the selfless way in which the Leader of the Opposition supports this motion, knowing that if anyone is to get a prize for being the best supporting actor it will be the Leader of the Opposition and that the Prime Minister has a great deal more to gain.

A Government of any political persuasion will have a natural tendency to prevent Parliament from exerting greater influence and power. In 1919, the House made the important decision to establish the Select Committee procedure to mirror the responsibilities of Government Departments and thereby enhance the power and influence of Parliament and hold the Government of the day more accountable. That balance of power seems to have slipped. The televising of Parliament and the greater coverage that that will certainly bring for Front Benchers and Back Benchers will constitutionally improve our ability to do what we are here to do, to represent the interests of our constituents and to hold accountable the Government of the day.

Mr. Eric S. Heffer (Liverpool, Walton): As another simple Member of Parliament, may I ask the Hon. Gentleman whether he agrees that such an experiment should be on the basis of a continuous channel, so that the House could be seen all the time when it is sitting? If the Hon. Gentleman cannot give us an assurance that that is what he believes, unless that is the view of the House, I shall not vote for this motion.

35

(Debate on the televising of parliamentary meetings:
Hansard, vol 127, col 194, 9 February 1988)

GLOSSARY

Hansard (heading) the official record of debates in the British Parliament

Hon (line 1) honourable (abbreviation), a traditional way of addressing Members of Parliament during meetings of the Parliament

concede (line 2) to accept a point of view; to agree

the Prime Minister (lines 2–3) refers to Margaret Thatcher, Prime Minister of Britain 1979–1990

unique (line 3) very special

the House (line 4) the House of Commons, the lower house of the British Parliament

Dispatch Box (line 6) the place where Ministers stand to make a statement to Parliament

Prime Minister's Questions (line 7) parliamentary time set aside for the addressing of specific questions to the Prime Minister

Hon Member (lines 8–9) a Member of Parliament

motion (line 14) an idea or proposal for discussion which will be voted on

supporting actor (line 16) an actor who does not play the main part

persuasion (line 18) a formal word for point of view

exert influence (lines 19–20) to influence

Select Committee (line 21) a small parliamentary committee appointed for a special purpose

procedure (line 22) a way of doing something

enhance (line 23) to improve

coverage (line 26) reporting in a newspaper, television or radio

Front Bencher (line 27) a leading member of the Government or Opposition parties

Back Bencher (line 27) a Member of Parliament not holding a senior office

constitutionally (line 28) according to the law and organization of the country

constituents (line 29) the voters who elect a Member of Parliament

hold accountable (line 30) to make sure that something is done properly and responsibly

continuous channel (line 34) a television channel which shows the same programme all the time

give an assurance (line 36) to promise something

GRAMMAR AND STYLE NOTE

The English used in British parliamentary discussion is normally very formal. Often verbs are used together with nouns rather than on their own. For example 'make a contribution' (line 3) (to contribute); 'exert influence' (line 19) (to influence); 'give an assurance' (line 36) (to assure).

LANGUAGE PRACTICE

A Put in the missing words. You can find all the words in the text. The first letters of the missing words are given.

1 The Prime Minister has made a u___ contribution to the country.
2 She is of a socialist political p___.
3 Is the televising of parliament the correct p___ for this country?
4 I can give an a___ that I will not vote for this motion.
5 Members of Parliament have to represent the interests of their c___.
6 We have everything to gain and little to l___ from this experiment.

B Answer the following questions. The answers to the questions all contain a specialized word or phrase. All the words appear in the text.

1 What is the book called in which debates in the British Parliament are recorded?
2 Where do Ministers stand to make a statement to Parliament?
3 What does the abbreviation MP stand for?
4 What is the word for an MP who holds senior office in the government?

C Discuss the following question with a partner who has read the text.
Should there be more political discussion on television? Give two reasons *why* and two reasons *why not*.

News Reporting and Journalism

11 PUTTING THE BITE ON BIG MAC

OUTLOOK
Pauline Springett

There is a McDonald's restaurant for every 26,000 people in the United States. The ratio in the UK is one for every 95,000 – leaving no doubt that the world's largest and most successful fast food chain has not finished expanding here.

Last year McDonald's announced its intention to double the number of restaurants in the UK within 10 years. The expansion would create 30,000 jobs, it boasted.

In 1994, McDonald's opened 57 restaurants, an investment in property, construction and equipment of £57 million.

That brought the chain's total investment in the UK since 1974 to just under £1 billion, a figure it will have exceeded by the end of this year. McDonald's opened its first restaurant in 1974 in Woolwich, South-east London. Twenty years later it employed more than 33,000 people, with a further 5,000 employed by franchises, and operated 570 UK restaurants.

The company is not listed on the UK Stock Exchange, although its accounts can be found at Companies House. Instead, befitting its origins, McDonald's is quoted in the US so it is tricky to assess UK finances and the company's annual review for 1994–95 has to serve.

It is a success story to be proud of. Who would have thought that McDonald's serves more than 1.2 million people in the UK 364 days a year?

(from *The Guardian*, 16 May 1995)

GLOSSARY

bite (heading) a small meal or a snack (noun); also to use your teeth (verb and noun)

Big Mac (heading) a large hamburger made by the McDonald's company

fast food (line 6) hot food that is prepared and served quickly after you order it

chain (line 6) a number of restaurants or shops owned by the same company

expand/expansion (line 6, 9) to grow in size

boast (line 9) to talk about something in a proud way

investment (lines 10–11) buying something so that you will make a profit

construction (line 11) buildings

exceed (line 15) to go beyond

franchise (line 18) someone who has an agreement with a company, allowing them to sell its goods or services

listed (line 20) put on an official list of public companies

stock exchange (line 20) a place where people buy and sell stocks and shares

accounts (line 21) a record of money spent

befitting (line 22) appropriate to

tricky (line 23) difficult

assess (line 23) to consider carefully

annual review (line 24) a year's statement of trading success

serve (line 24) 'the review has to serve', the review is all there is

serve (line 26) 'McDonald's serves more than . . .', to give food or goods to people

LANGUAGE PRACTICE

A   Put in the missing words. You can find all the words in the text. The first letters of the missing words are given.

   1   The most successful fast food ch____ will now ex____ even further.

   2   The company has announced its in____ to double the number of r____.

3   The company has invested in equipment, property and con___.
4   It is tr___ to assess the company's finances.
5   The company is very pr___ of its success and b___ about its success.
6   The company s___ 1.2 million people per day.

B   Substitute the underlined words with a word or words from the text. Make any grammatical changes which are necessary.

1   Last year McDonald's said that it is intended to have twice the number of UK restaurants within ten years.
2   The company will continue to expand here.
3   It is the biggest fast food chain and has had the most success.
4   It is a story of success to take pride in.

C   Write a brief paragraph (50 words) discussing why fast food restaurants are so popular throughout the world.

12   BOOK REVIEW

A LONG WAY TO LINGUISTICS
Wild Swans by Jung Chang

Review by John McRae

What makes a book a best seller? If you look at the best-selling lists in the Sunday papers you will find the big names like Ken Follett and Jeffrey Archer, Joanna Trollope and Catherine Cookson. These are novelists who always seem to be somewhere on the lists.

But they don't stay on the lists for very long – three or four months is a good run for a best seller in paperback. So it is a surprise to find a book of nearly 700 pages by a

Chinese woman, Jung Chang, which has been at or near the top of the lists for a *year* and four months.

This unexpected hit is *Wild Swans*, 'Three Daughters of China'. It is as exciting to read as any thriller or saga by more famous Western writers. It is a true story – and truth is often stranger than fiction. Jung Chang tells the story of her grandmother, her mother, and herself, and in so doing tells an amazing, very involving story of the survival of a family, as well as telling the complex and often confusing history of modern China.

For a long time I resisted the temptation to follow the crowd and read this book. I thought it might be cashing in on the success of Amy Tan's very enjoyable *The Joy Luck Club* and hit movies from China such as *The Wedding Banquet* and *Farewell My Concubine*. I was wrong – this is a great book. I am tempted to quote scene after scene, but I would go on for ever. It is one of these books that make you take the phone off the hook, sit up reading all night, miss meals and appointments. It is full of pain – the sufferings of these women are terrible. From the pain of broken feet (to make a woman's feet small and 'attractive' her bones were deliberately broken), through the agony of political alienation, through solitude, famine, exile, all the pain is turned towards triumph.

For *Wild Swans* is ultimately a story of survival. Jung Chang managed to get to Britain and complete a PhD in linguistics. How many of us have got our qualifications after a journey like hers? She tells us the whole story; she was a Red Guard, a peasant, a 'barefoot doctor', a steel-worker, and an electrician. All of these before studying English and starting her academic career.

Every reader will be humbled by this book – and deeply moved. I am reminded of Edgar's words at the end of Shakespeare's *King Lear*: 'we that are young shall never see so much, nor live so long.'

Read it – and think of your own journeys to where you are now. You will find sentences, pages, episodes,

⁵⁰ whole chapters that your students will respond to: how different from their own lives it all is, but how close to us all in the depths of its humanity.

Jung Chang's was a long road to a degree in English – but she has shared it with the world, and given us a masterpiece. A Wonderful Book.

⁵⁵
John McRae

(Unpublished book review by John McRae, October 1994)

GLOSSARY

linguistics (line 1) the academic study of language
best seller (line 4) a book of which large numbers of copies have been sold
hit (line 14) a record, play, film or book that has become very successful
thriller (line 15) an exciting or sensational story or play
saga (line 15) a long story, often giving the history of a family
involving (line 19) makes you feel you are taking part in things
survival (line 19) continuing to exist
complex (line 20) difficult to understand
resist the temptation (line 22) not to give in to your feelings
banquet (line 25) a very grand meal
concubine (line 26) a female lover (not a modern word)
alienation (line 34) a feeling of being alone with your own feelings and ideas
solitude (line 34) loneliness
famine (line 34) a serious shortage of food
exile (line 34) being forced to live away from your own country
PhD (line 37) 'doctor of philosophy' (abbreviation), the highest academic qualification
peasant (line 40) someone who works on the land in a poor country
Red Guard (line 40) a member of a militant youth movement in China (1966–76)
humbled (line 43) to feel that you are not valuable or important
degree (line 53) a university course and qualification

LANGUAGE PRACTICE

A Put in the missing words. You can find all the words in the text. The first letters of the missing words are given.

   1 A very successful book is called a b____ s____.
   2 The book was an unexpected h____.
   3 The story of the history of modern China is often confusing and c____.
   4 The author completed a P____ degree in linguistics.
   5 The author lived a life of solitude and political al____.
   6 I was humbled and deeply m____ by this book.

B Substitute the underlined words with a word or words from the text. Make any grammatical changes which are necessary.

   1 What makes a book which sells very well?
   2 The book tells the story of a family which survived.
   3 It is a book which makes you not answer the phone.
   4 It is tempting to describe lots of different scenes from the book.

C Write a brief summary (about 50 words) of the life of Jung Chang.

---

13 SPORTS REPORT: BASKETBALL

MAGIC – POOF! – MAKE JORDAN AND HIS BULLS DISAPPEAR
by Michael Wilbon
Washington Post Service
NBA PLAYOFFS

CHICAGO – The looks on the faces of the Chicago Bulls said they couldn't believe it.

With just more than three minutes left, they had led by eight points and a Game 7 of their NBA Eastern Conference semifinal appeared inevitable. But the young Orlando Magic stormed back in a way Michael Jordan and the Bulls used to.

They scored the last 14 points of the game while Jordan shot an air ball and made two questionable passes in the final 30 seconds. And that improbable combination of events gave Orlando a 108–102 victory that eliminated the Bulls, 4 games to 2.

It was the first time since 1990, in Game 7 against the then-defending champion Detroit Pistons, that the Bulls with Jordan had walked off the court as losers in a playoff series.

But when Orlando's Shaquille O'Neal dunked home the final two points with just seconds remaining, it served to underscore that the Magic are younger, stronger, quicker, perhaps smarter and indisputably better. It was their second victory here in the United Center, and the third game in this series in which Jordan was shaky down the stretch.

With 3:24 left, after B J Armstrong's 3-pointer put the Bulls up, 102–94, it seemed the series was headed back to Orlando. Instead, the Magic got an offensive rebound basket from O'Neal, a 3-pointer from Nick Anderson and two free throws from Brian Shaw, then a shake-and-bake jumper from Anderson with 42.8 seconds left that put them ahead, 103–102.

Jordan had missed everything with his shot when the Bulls were ahead, 102–101, and it had become obvious several minutes earlier that he was exceptionally tired. After Anderson's go-ahead basket, the Bulls called time out.

(from *The International Herald Tribune*, 20/21 May 1995)

GLOSSARY

NBA (line 5) National Basketball Association (abbreviation)

playoff (line 5) extra games played to decide the winner of a sports competition when two or more teams have the same score

Chicago Bulls (line 6) a basketball team from Chicago, USA

inevitable (line 10) something that has to happen

Orlando Magic (line 10) a basketball team from Orlando, USA

stormed back (line 11) fought back powerfully

questionable (line 12) not absolutely certain; something is not quite right

improbable (line 15) unlikely to happen

combination (line 15) two or more events or people working together

eliminated (line 16) in sport, to be defeated and to take no further part in the competition

dunked home (line 22) dropped the ball in the basket or net

underscore (line 24) to emphasize, to stress

smart (line 25) (American English) clever

indisputably (line 25) without doubt

shaky (line 27) nervous, uncertain

down the stretch (lines 27–28) in the final part of the game

rebound basket (lines 31–32) a basket (see below) in which the ball bounces off the board at the back of the net

shake-and-bake jumper (lines 33–34) a basket (see below) in which the basket (net) shakes

basket (line 39) the word 'basket' has two main meanings. It refers to the net into which a ball is placed in order to score points in the game of basketball. It also refers to a point in basketball. A team can win by 101 baskets (points) to 93

time out (line 39) a brief pause in the game

GRAMMAR AND STYLE NOTE

The title of the report plays with words. 'Poof!' is a word used by magicians when they make things disappear. Magic is also the name of the team Orlando Magic. They play so well that they make the other team, The Bulls, disappear.

LANGUAGE PRACTICE

A Put in the missing words. You can find all the words in the text. The first letters of the missing words are given.

1 He was rather nervous and sh____ and his decisions were qu____.
2 They lost the match and were el____.
3 The result under____ that the younger team were the better team.
4 An im____ combination of events gave them victory.
5 In____ the best team won.
6 The whole team were ex____ tired.

B Answer the following questions. The answers to the questions all contain a specialist word or phrase. All the words appear in the text.

1 What is the spelling of 'centre' (British English) in American English?
2 What is the name given to a successful shot or score in basketball?
3 What are the initials for National Basketball Association?
4 What is the word for a score in basketball when the player drops the ball into the basket?

C Write a brief paragraph (about 50 words) saying what your favourite sport is and why.

---

14 SPORTS REPORT: FOOTBALL

PALMER SHOOTS DOWN WARBLING CANARIES
John Wilford at Elland Road

· Leeds United   2
McAllister 80(pen), Palmer 90
Norwich City   1
Ward 36   Att: 31, 982

42

NORWICH players – hot, angry and disappointed at the end of this close encounter – surrounded referee Wilkie with, it must be said, some cause.

After being handed the lead in farcical style, they then succumbed to a bitterly disputed penalty and an injury-time goal. So down they go while Leeds stay on target for a return to Europe. Good luck to them. They certainly had it aplenty in this match. After a tentative start, City fought like tigers and a draw or a win would have been fair reward. Credit Leeds, though, for staying power. They are lethal in the final quarter of a match.

In contrast to the lethargy they had shown the previous week against Aston Villa, Leeds looked decidedly frisky from the outset. McAllister and Deane pushed deep into City's defence and former Elland Road stalwart Newcome was given some anxious moments. Then in the 36th minute, Leeds gave away the lead. It was as daft a goal as you will see in a season. Goss played an optimistic through ball into the heart of the Leeds back line. Wetherall and Pemberton were under mild threat from Akinibyi but left the ball to Lukic, who was rushing from goal. Unfortunately the keeper was unsighted by Kelly running across him and missed the ball completely. All Ward had to do was take a leisurely walk into an open net.

Leeds were being forced deep into their own half when they desperately wanted to break forward. But they were offered a hope of saving the game or better with Mr Wilkie's generosity. The penalty he awarded was pretty dodgy. McAllister scored from the spot.

There were ten minutes left and Leeds looked much more interested in scoring than defending. They were often out-numbered as Norwich hit them on the break, but it looked worth the risk as first Deane and then Whelan twice went agonisingly close. Norwich's number eventually came up in the 90th minute when Palmer repeated his heroics of the previous week, poking home Speed's cross from the corner flag.

(from *The Observer*, 7 May 1995)

GLOSSARY

warble (line 1) birdsong

Canaries (line 1) a nickname for Norwich City. A canary is a
   small yellow bird

80, 90, 36 (lines 4 and 6) the minute in a ninety-minute match
   when a goal was scored

pen (*penalty*) (line 4) the chance to score a goal without being
   prevented by other players, given when a member of the other
   team commits a foul (for example, injures another player).
   Abbreviation is 'pen'

att (line 6) attendance (abbreviation). The number of spectators
   at the match

encounter (line 8) meeting of two people or teams

farcical (line 10) very comical

disputed (line 11) disagreed with

injury time (lines 11–12) extra time played in a match to make up for
   time lost when someone was hurt

Europe (line 13) 'Europe' here means, European cup football
   competitions

tentative (line 14) uncertain, not confident

staying power (line 16) determination

lethal (line 17) very dangerous

lethargy (line 18) tiredness

frisky (line 19) energetic

stalwart (line 21) loyal

anxious (line 22) nervous

daft (line 23) stupid or silly (an informal word)

the Leeds back line (line 25) the defensive members of the team

unsighted (line 28) prevented from seeing

dodgy (line 35) uncertain (an informal word)

the spot (line 35) the point on the ground from which penalties
   are taken

went close (lines 39–40) narrowly missed

agonizingly (line 40) painfully

heroics (line 41) brave actions

poking (line 42) kicking

cross (line 42) a pass high in the air

Metaphors are common in sports reports; the metaphors are often of war and battle and can describe sports contests in quite violent language. Notice here the metaphors 'shoot down' (line 1); 'lethal' (line 17); 'threat' (line 26); 'outnumber' (lines 37–8) as well as standard sports words such as 'attack' and 'defend'.

LANGUAGE PRACTICE

A   Put in the missing words. You can find all the words in the text. The first letters of the missing words are given.

1   The team were l____ in the final part of the match but were anx____ at the beginning.
2   After a t____ start, the whole team fought like tigers.
3   The first goal was farcical and d____.
4   They looked much more interested in scoring than def____.
5   Ag____, they nearly scored twice.
6   The referee's decision was pretty d____.

B   Answer the following questions. The answers to the questions all contain a specialist word or phrase. All the words appear in the text.

1   What is the word used in football when the team has a chance to score a goal 'from the spot'?
2   What is the abbreviation for 'penalty'?
3   What is the abbreviation for the attendance (the number of spectators at the match)?
4   What are the words used for extra time played in a match because players have been injured?

C   Write a paragraph (about 50 words) saying why you think football is such a popular game throughout the world.

15 SOARAWAY PSION

1 SALES SURGE SPURS SOARAWAY PSION

A BULLISH agm statement from Psion chairman David
Potter sent shares of the hand-held computer group 7p
higher to a five-year peak of 324p.

Potter told shareholders that sales in the first four
months 'have shown a substantial increase'. He gave no
figures, but industry sources believe the increase could be
anything up to 30pc.

Demand is strong for the new one and two megabyte
Series 3a models – the latter will cost you more than £300
– and Psion would like to turn out more. The problem is
supply of the vital memory chips.

(from *The Daily Telegraph*, 6 May 1995)

GLOSSARY

surge (line 1) a sudden increase

spur (line 1) to encourage

soaraway (line 1) an adjective formed from the verb 'to soar
 away'; that is, to fly to a great height

bullish (line 2) trying to cause a rise in prices on the Stock
 Exchange

AGM (line 2) annual general meeting (abbreviation)

hand-held computer (line 3) a small computer that can be carried
 around

peak (line 4) the highest level or value

shareholders (line 5) someone who owns shares. (Shares are parts
 of a company which individuals can buy as an investment)

substantial (line 6) very large

sources (line 7) people with necessary information

megabyte (line 9) a million bytes, a measure of the power of
 computers

turn out (line 11) to manufacture

vital (line 12) very important

chips (line 12) microchips, small pieces of (usually silicon) semi-conductors which carry electronic circuits.

GRAMMAR AND STYLE NOTES

1 Headlines to newspaper articles often use creative and striking language. Here there is a 'poetic' pattern of repeated 's' sounds.

2 Headlines are also often characterized by simple, one-syllable words 'sales surge spurs . . .' and by a simple present tense of the verb, even though past events are being reported.

LANGUAGE PRACTICE

A Put in the missing words. You can find all the words in the text. The first letters of the missing words are given.

1 The d____ for the new computers is strong.
2 The company would like to t____ o____ more.
3 Industry s____ believe that the increases in sales could be even higher next year.
4 The increase in sales has been sub____.
5 The memory chips are v____.
6 Shares have reached a p____ of 324p.

B Substitute the underlined words with a word or words from the text. Make any grammatical changes which are necessary.

1 The chairman made an <u>optimistic statement at the Annual General Meeting</u>.
2 The problem is supply of <u>memory chips which are very important</u>.
3 There was a sudden <u>increase</u> in sales.
4 The company would like <u>to manufacture more computers which you can hold in your hand</u>.

C List three main advantages of hand-held computers.

16 EDITORIAL

INTERNATIONAL HERALD TRIBUNE
Published with the New York Times and the Washington Post

A PATTERN OF DUPLICITY

America's relations with Guatemala are a chilling study in cynicism. Beginning with a 1954 coup engineered by the CIA, Cold War security concerns dictated nearly every aspect of the relationship with this impoverished country. Abuses by Guatemalan military and security services went unchecked, and Americans who wandered into the way were killed or tortured with barely a protest from Washington.

The latest case to come to light seems to fit the pattern. As The New York Times has reported, Peter Tiscione, an archaeologist, was found dead in his hotel room in Guatemala in 1992 shortly after calling his wife in New York to tell her he feared for his life. The U.S. Embassy quickly accepted the Guatemalan government's glib explanation that he had stabbed himself in the neck four times with a machete.

Mr. Tiscione is hardly the first American to die in mysterious circumstances in Guatemala, or the first to be callously neglected by the State Department. In 1976 five Americans were killed in a plane crash. The official explanations – first bad weather, then engine failure – turned out to be false. Several witnesses said they had seen soldiers shoot down the plane.

All these cases have in common a well-founded suspicion of military wrongdoing and a timid State Department response. Representative Robert Torricelli, who made public the CIA's involvement in the murder of Ms. Harbury's husband, has documented 20 cases of Americans who were killed or subjected to human rights abuses in Guatemala.

Americans deserve a truthful accounting of the events

of the past 40 years in Guatemala. Guatemalans deserve no less. Americans also deserve a diplomatic service that looks after their interests and refuses to tolerate the complicity of 35 foreign governments in their mistreatment.

(from *The International Herald Tribune*, 20/21 May 1995)

GLOSSARY

duplicity (line 3) a speech or action which tries to make us believe something which is not true

chilling (line 4) cold

cynicism (line 5) a belief that people always behave selfishly

coup (line 5) when a group of people seize power in a country, usually with violence

CIA (line 6) the Central Intelligence Agency of America (abbreviation)

cold war (line 6) a state of extreme hostility between two nations, without actual fighting

dictated (line 6) controlled

impoverished (line 7) very poor

abuse (line 8) actions in which people do wrong

unchecked (line 9) not controlled

tortured (line 10) treated very cruelly

Washington (line 11) the capital and centre of government in the USA

come to light (line 12) to be made known

archaeologist (line 14) someone who studies the history of ancient cultures

glib explanation (line 17) when something is explained so easily that it cannot be trusted

machete (line 18) a large knife with a broad blade

callous (line 20) cold and unfeeling

well-founded (line 26) strong, firmly-based

timid (line 27) fearful

representative (line 28) someone who is chosen to make decisions and speak on behalf of others

documented (line 30) written about something in a detailed, factual way *tolerate* (line 35) to allow something to happen even if you may not agree with it

complicity (line 35) an involvement in something that is wrong or not lawful

LANGUAGE PRACTICE

A Put in the missing words. You can find all the words in the text. The first letters of the missing words are given.

1 The attacks on this im____ country led to serious ab____.
2 New information has come to l____.
3 No one could trust such a g____ story.
4 Many people were killed and cruelly t____.
5 They were subjected to abuses of human r____.
6 The complicity of foreign governments cannot be t____.

B Substitute the underlined words with a word or words from the text. Make any grammatical changes which are necessary.

1 There was a suspicion that the military had acted wrongly. People found it was true.
2 He feared that he would die.
3 The representative brought the murder to the attention of the public.
4 He was not the first American who died in circumstances which nobody could understand.

C Write a brief paragraph (about 50 words) in which you give two reasons why there is sometimes a cold war between countries.

17 CHILDREN AND CARTOONS

For many years now parents, teachers and individual members of the community have been interested and concerned
about what children and young people read. Books have   5
been written, surveys compiled and 'recommended' book-
lists printed. Research within this area has been vital for
those actively involved in choosing positive anti-racist and
anti-sexist resources. However, this interest in what children
read and how it influences them, has not been balanced   10
with an interest for what children watch on television.

Children's TV has changed and developed over the
last 10 years and in some ways the quality of the programmes has improved. Gone are the days of 'Andy
Pandy', 'Crackerjack' and 'Thunderbirds'. Instead a new   15
brand of TV exists for more children and for more
hours of the day.

The introduction of American-based cartoons such as
He-Man, She-Ra, Thundercats and Ulysses 21 now
dominate our TV screens, similarly the toys and item-   20
related products crowd our shops. Children insist that their
lunch boxes feature Skeletor, or their duvet cover has to
have She-Ra. The product-related material is endless as is
the children's demand for it. These new brands of cartoon
depict a violent storyline, which, for the most part is filled 25
with throw-away lines spoken by larger-than-life characters. All in all the cartoons are badly animated, incredibly
complex to comprehend (apart from the tedious fighting
scenes) and very boring to watch. However, it is far too
easy to simply dismiss these cartoons as 'bad' television, 30
because the many messages contained within such programmes are both subtle and insidious.

Within all of the cartoons the racist imagery and

overtones are unmistakable. The heroes and heroines and the
35 defenders of the 'good' are white. They boast blonde hair,
blue eyes and sun-tanned faces. The female characters are
usually scantily clad, with wasp like waists, which perpetu-
ate an image of beauty that is most definitely white and
European. She-Ra's long blonde flowing hair and blue eyes
40 are of course complemented by 'He-Man's' tanned, over-
developed muscles, his mass of tidy, but wavy hair and yet
again his strong, blue, piercing eyes. The 'baddies' however,
are nearly always shrouded in darkness, dressed in black or
grey costumes and inhabit dark and gloomy caves usually
45 below the ground's surface. Often the characters are not
depicted as 'Black' but they are never depicted as white.

On a recent 'Right to Reply' programme (August
1987) where the topic of such cartoons was discussed at
length, the creator of 'He-Man' stated that 'as there were
50 no black heroes then there should be no black baddies'.
Some may say that's an acceptable statement, but why are
there no black heroes and secondly why are the 'baddies'
never depicted as white? In one episode of 'He-Man and
the Masters of the Universe' a character called 'Mumrah' (a
55 revived Egyptian mummy) was depicted as black and ugly.
The character has a large, broad nose, full lips and large
wide eyes. There was no doubt that in the eyes of the
creators ugliness and evilness are related to non-European
features. In other words the image of ugliness that they had
60 created was based on African/Afro Caribbean features.

(from *Dragon's Teeth*, no 28)

GLOSSARY

cult (line 1) an idea or activity which has become very popular
 and fashionable
vital (line 7) very important
anti-racist (line 8) to be against treating people as inferior because
 of their race

anti-sexist (line 9) to be against treating a man or a woman as inferior because of their gender

resources (line 9) something which you need or can refer to when you need information or support

Andy Pandy (lines 14–15) a 1950s British Programme with puppets, featuring the adventures of a group of toys, for preschool children

Crackerjack (line 15) a British programme in the 1950s and 1960s for schoolchildren, with games and features

Thunderbirds (line 15) a 1960s adventure series with puppets, featuring an organization called 'International Rescue'

item-related (lines 20–21) products which you can buy in shops which are connected with the cartoon in some way

duvet (line 22) a large cotton bag filled with material which keeps you warm. Used on a bed

throw-away lines (line 26) very casual, unimportant words

insidious (line 32) something which develops slowly and without being noticed, usually unpleasant

scantily clad (line 37) not wearing many clothes

wasp like waists (line 37) very narrow waists

complemented (line 40) closely matched

piercing (line 42) very sharp. Seeing things with piercing eyes is to see things very clearly

shrouded (line 43) hidden

Right to Reply (line 47) a British Channel 4 TV programme which invites viewers to criticize other programmes

revived (line 55) brought back to life

mummy (line 55) a person whose body has been preserved after they have died, usually in ancient Egypt

LANGUAGE PRACTICE

A Put in the missing words. In each case the first letters of the missing words are given. All the expressions are taken from the text.

  1 Cartoons now d____ our TV screens.
  2 The cartoons always have a v____ storyline and l____-than-l____ characters.

3 The messages contained within such programmes are s____.
4 The racism in such cartoons is un____.
5 The bad characters are nearly always dressed in black and inhabit g____ caves.
6 Ugliness and ev____ in these cartoons are related to non-European features.

B Substitute the underlined words with a word or words from the text. Make any grammatical changes which are necessary.

1 These new brands of cartoon have a violent plot.
2 The racist imagery and overtones are very clear to everyone.
3 The cartoons are badly animated and are extremely difficult to understand.
4 We cannot simply take no notice of such films. It is far too easy.

C Questions for discussion:

1 Are you influenced by the images in cartoons? Does it matter if the main characters have a white skin and blonde hair or a brown skin and black hair?
2 Do children watch too many cartoons? What are the advantages and disadvantages of cartoons?

18 POP MUSIC REVIEW

ROCK RECORDS
Sidi Bou Said Bodies (Ultimate)
Robert Cray Some Rainy Morning (Mercury)

CHARLES SHAAR MURRAY
This may be the last year in which the 'women in rock'

issue will remain worthy of discussion. Thanks to the likes of Bjök, Tanya Donnelly, Courtney Love, Tori Amos, Liz Phair, Justin Frischmann, L7 and Polly Harvey, women are finally no longer novelties, oddities or tokens; they're *here* once and for all.

Anyone still surprised by female presence on a contemporary rock stage not only hasn't been listening to rock, but probably lives underneath one. And now there's Sidi Bou Said.

The name may indeed imply some exciting new *rai* singer from Algeria, but, in fact, it belongs to a trio from exotic New Cross, south east London, whose second album finds them heading into some intriguing territory.

Despite low-key interventions from a string quartet and a fistful of recorders, Sidi Bou Said stick with bass and drums but wring new shapes and textures from them. The song structures are unpredictable, as they stop and start or shift tempo and texture; and the lyrics explore female sexuality in ways that no male fantasist ever would – or could.

With most leading boy groups content to recycle old postures inherited from Bowie, Morrissey or the Small Faces, the girls are the ones currently setting rock's pace, and with *Bodies*, Sidi Bou Said are well up with the frontrunners.

There is still plenty of space for artists using a traditional genre to carve out territory of their own. Robert Cray may have abandoned his populist approach of the second half of the Eighties, but he still dominates his own distinctive niche – a mixture of deep soul and blues.

Nowadays, producing his records and writing more of his own material, he's more the auteur than ever. His latest album is as raw and spontaneous as he has ever come in the studio, with the richest and most soulful singing and the spikiest, angriest guitar of his entire career.

(from *The Daily Telegraph*, 6 May 1995)

GLOSSARY

tokens (line 9) a symbol of something rather than the real thing

trio (line 16) a group of three

exotic (line 17) something unusual from far away

album (line 17) a record with about thirty minutes of music on each side

intriguing (line 18) interesting

low key (line 19) not really noticed or not attracting much attention

intervention (line 19) to join in, to take part in

string quartet (line 19) a group of four people playing violins and other string instruments

fistful (line 20) a colloquial expression, meaning a number of

recorder (line 20) a musical instrument similar to a flute

stick with (line 20) continue with

bass (line 20) bass guitar, an instrument typically used in producing a 'pop' sound

wring (line 21) to squeeze out – here meaning create

unpredictable (line 22) unexpected, unconventional

tempo (line 23) musical word for 'speed'

fantasist (line 24) someone who imagines things that they hope will happen

postures (line 26) poses or attitudes which people assume to achieve a certain effect

Bowie (line 26) David Bowie, an influential 1960s–90s rock singer

Morrissey (line 26) the songwriter and lead singer of The Smiths, a contemporary rock group

Small Faces (lines 26–27) a 1960s pop group

setting the pace (line 27) to lead, to make something new

front-runners (lines 28–29) the leaders

genre (line 31) a style or form in music, art and literature

distinctive (lines 33–34) easy to recognize

niche (line 34) a position which is exactly suitable for someone

soul (line 34) music incorporating rhythm and blues and gospel music, the product of American Black culture

blues (line 34) melancholic music of American Black folk origin

auteur (line 36) a French word meaning author

spontaneous (line 37) something that is not planned and is lively and natural

spikiest (line 39) spiky means to have sharp points; it also means bad-tempered

LANGUAGE PRACTICE

A Put in the missing words. You can find all the words in the text. The first letters of the missing words are given.

   1 The 'women in rock' issue will remain w___ of discussion.

   2 Women are no longer novelties or o___ in rock music.

   3 Their second a___ finds them heading into some new territory.

   4 Their song structures are un___ and unusual.

   5 Now he is producing his own records and writing more of his own ma___

   6 His latest album is raw and s___.

B Substitute the underlined words with a word or words from the text. Make any grammatical changes which are necessary.

   1 Because of the likes of Björk and other female singers women are no longer novelties.

   2 The girls are the ones currently out in front in rock.

   3 They're here for ever.

   4 The album was made by a group of three.

C Write a brief paragraph (about 50 words) in which you describe your favourite rock or pop music album.

19 DOW DAMPENS ASIA MARKETS

Reuters

HONG KONG – The biggest fall in the Dow Jones industrial average in six months Thursday dragged down most Asian stock markets Friday, although some recovered late in the day to end with only moderate losses.

Key indexes in Hong Kong, Manila, Kuala Lumpur, Seoul, Bangkok, Sydney and Wellington finished sharply lower. Many brokers pointed to the fall on Wall Street, but others attributed the losses to corrections after big gains last week.

The Dow fell 81.96 points, to 4,340.64, in its biggest one-day drop since Nov. 22, 1994.

'Wall Street exacerbated a correction that we started to see in the last days,' said John Quinn, chief investment officer at NatWest Investment Management Asia in Hong Kong.

But he said Asian markets were supported by bullish earnings, gross domestic product growth and the prospect of steady U.S. interest rates.

The Nikkei 225 average lost 171.71 points, or 1.05 percent, to 16,140.85.

In Hong Kong, the blue-chip Hang Seng index, which had gained more than 1,000 points in two weeks, fell 102.40 points, or 1.12 percent, to 9,013.32.

Singapore's 30-share Straits Times Industrials index recovered from an early decline to end down 4.54 points, or 0.21 percent, at 2,158.93.

'I would expect New York to continue correcting, maybe not as sharply,' one dealer said.

(from *The International Herald Tribune*, 20/21 May 1995)

GLOSSARY

Dow (heading) the Dow Jones Index – a figure which indicates the relative price of shares on the New York Stock Exchange. Other indexes are the Nikkei (line 20) in Tokyo, and the Hang Seng (line 22) in Hong Kong

dampen (heading) to make something less lively and active

industrial average (lines 2–3) the average performance of the main shares in the stock exchange

moderate (line 5) neither large nor small

broker (line 8) a person who buys and sells shares, foreign money or goods on behalf of other people

Wall Street (line 8) the American money market

corrections (line 9) the market corrects when brokers judge that share prices have risen or fallen too fast

exacerbate (line 13) to make something worse

bullish (line 17) share prices begin to rise and big profits can be made

gross domestic product (line 18) the total goods made and sold within a country

blue-chip (line 22) something of very high quality

end down (line 26) at the end of the day's trading the index of prices is lower or down

LANGUAGE PRACTICE

A Put in the missing words. You can find all the words in the text. The first letters of the missing words are given.

1 Share prices re____ to end with only moderate losses.
2 There has been a f____ in share prices on Wall Street.
3 The k____ indexes are in Hong Kong, Singapore and Tokyo.
4 There is a good prospect of st____ interest rates.
5 There were corrections in the Dow Jones Index after big g____ last week.
6 The performance of the Dow has da____ Asia markets.

B Answer the following questions. The answers to the questions all contain a specialist word or phrase. All the words appear in the text.

1 What is the word used to describe a market when share prices begin to rise and profits can be made?

2 What is the name given to a person who buys and sells stocks and shares for others?

3 What is the word which describes something of very high quality?

4 Name three international stock exchanges.

C With a partner who has read the text, give three reasons why people like to gamble (for example, on horses, the stock exchange, in casinos, etc).

Magazine Language

20 HOROSCOPE

TAURUS
April 21–May 21
You may need to defend yourself against an unfair accusation this week. That would be simple if it weren't for the fact that you feel guilty about something you've done – and probably ought not to have. That, however, is a totally separate issue. See a link and you'll do no favours to yourself or anyone else for that matter. Forget it and just seize this week's opportunity to move away from regret towards a far more satisfying future.

CANCER
June 23–July 23
Mars is still in your sign. Until early October you'll continue to feel a strong urge to force certain issues, shake certain sleepy people into a state of wakefulness – and generally do all you can to seize every chance you have to make your world a better place. You're right to be pushy while you have this opportunity – but you must be careful what you push for . . . and who you push in order to get it. You owe it to yourself to be very selective and discriminating.

VIRGO
Aug 24–Sep 23
You should now be looking at life through a different pair of spectacles. The new ones are clearer, more comfortable and, even if they do have a slightly rosy tint, it's only enough to provide the optimism you'll need to make the kind of progress you now must strive for. Don't be disappointed if your first attempts to move in a new direction fall a little flat this week. Try again – and again, if necessary. But don't worry – you'll get there!

CAPRICORN
Dec 22–Jan 20
You may have to spend much of the week wrestling with
a practical problem that seems determined not to go away.
It's likely to involve a distinct difference of opinion, a need   35
to speak plainly to someone who probably doesn't want to
hear what you want to say – and the search for a new
arrangement that will keep everyone happy in the longer
term. Unfortunately there's no simple solution, but if you
persevere I'm sure you'll win through in the end.   40

(from 'Your Stars' by Jonathan Cainer, *Woman* magazine,
May 1994)

GLOSSARY

horoscope (heading) what will happen in the future under a
    particular sign of the Zodiac
Taurus, Cancer, Virgo and Capricorn (lines 1, 11, 21 and 31) signs
    of the Zodiac
accusation (lines 3–4) the act of showing or saying that you think
    someone has done something bad or wrong
do no favours to yourself (lines 7–8) *not* to give yourself any
    advantage
regret (line 9) a feeling of sadness and disappointment
urge (line 14) a strong desire to do or to have something
pushy (line 17) someone who wants to be better than others and
    can be very rude
discriminating (line 20) someone who chooses or judges things
    very carefully
spectacles (line 24) a formal rather old-fashioned word for
    'glasses'
rosy (line 25) to see through 'rosy' or 'rose-tinted' spectacles is to
    be unrealistically happy
fall flat (line 29) to fail, not to succeed
wrestling (line 33) to try to work out how to solve a difficult
    problem
persevere (line 40) to keep trying very hard to do something

1 Notice how horoscopes end on a positive note and offer advice which expresses clear positive values. You can learn many positive words (as well as lots of words for evaluating things) by reading horoscopes, especially the conclusions to individual horoscopes. Note here, for example, the words 'seize the opportunity'; 'selective and discriminating'; 'you'll get there!'; 'you'll win through'.

2 Modal verbs and imperatives are common in horoscopes since they allow the writer to estimate, judge, advise and recommend for example, 'should' 'must' 'may' 'will' – informally ' 'll'. Notice imperatives such as 'see'; 'forget'; 'try'; 'don't'.

3 A similar style can be found in 'Problem Pages' and 'Advice' articles – see pp. 70 and 74.

LANGUAGE PRACTICE

A Put in the missing words. You can find all the words in the text. The first letters of the missing words are given.

   1 He made a very unfair acc____ against me.
   2 S____ an opportunity to do better in the future.
   3 You should try to be more selective and dis____.
   4 Don't be disappointed if all your plans f____ flat.
   5 Try not to wr____ with these problems for too long.
   6 There's no simple sol____ but you must per____.

B Substitute the underlined words with a word or words from the text. Make any grammatical changes which are necessary.

   1 Until October you'll <u>very much want to</u> force certain issues.
   2 I spent most of the week <u>trying very hard to work out how to solve</u> a practical problem.
   3 We hope the new arrangement will keep everyone happy <u>in the future</u>.
   4 I'm sure you'll <u>finally succeed</u>.

C Write a horoscope entry for yourself in which you predict what will happen to you in the next week. Write about 30 words and make sure you say everything that you really want to happen to you.

21 JUST TESTING (WOKS)

FRY AND MIGHTY
Our experts put woks to the test

Argos *Traditional Chinese Wok Set*, £9.50 Lightweight
model, easily lifted with two handles. Steel wok comes   5
with lid, cooking chopsticks, chopsticks, metal scoop/
spatula, wooden rice paddle, steamer rack, tempura rack,
support ring. Stable to use, seasoned well. Racks quite
flimsy, but performance not affected. Weight 1lb 7¾oz
(740g), diameter 12in (30cm).   **Rating (out of five):★★★**   10

Boots *Oriental Wok Set*, £14.99 Good gift idea. Carbon
steel wok with single wooden handle. Comes with lid, tempura rack, steaming rack, cooking chopsticks, spatula,
recipe book, chopsticks. Seasoned well; good quality accessories. Balancing loop would be useful. Weight 2lb 2oz   15
(1.1kg), diameter 12in (30cm). **Best performance and
value for money   Rating:★★★★★**

Meyer *Chinese Style Wok*, £21.99 Comfortable to use
and gave good results. Aluminium wok with Teflon   2
non-stick interior and enamel exterior and lid. Single heat- 20
resistant handle, useful hanging loop. Comes with metal
steam rack, bamboo steam rack, tempura rack, cooking
chopsticks and spatula chopsticks. Weight 1lb 8¼oz (760g),
diameter 12½in (31cm).   **Rating:★★★★**

Meyer *Electric Wok,* approx. £39.99 Heated up quickly   25
and temperature easily controlled. Aluminium wok with
SilverStone non-stick interior, enamelled exterior and lid.
Cannot be used on a hob. Accessories include metal

tempura rack, wooden steam rack, chopsticks, cooking chop-
30   sticks and spatula. Weight 2lb 7$\frac{1}{4}$oz (1.2kg), diameter 14in
(35cm).   **Rating:★★★★**

(from *The Daily Mail*, 24 September 1994)

GLOSSARY

fry and mighty (line 2) you fry things in a wok. The phrase
    'high and mighty' means very important. The title of the
    article plays on words with similar sounds (fry – high)
wok (line 3) a bowl-shaped frying pan used in (especially)
    Chinese cookery
chopsticks (line 6) sticks of wood or ivory, used as eating utensils
    by the Chinese or Japanese
scoop/spatula (lines 6–7) an object like a knife with a very wide,
    flat blade used in cooking
tempura (line 7) a Japanese dish of fish, shellfish or vegetables,
    very lightly fried
seasoned well (line 7) still good quality after being used many
    times
flimsy (line 9) something weak or badly made
diameter (line 10) the distance of a straight line drawn through
    the middle of a circle
rating (line 10) another word for mark out of five or ten (here
    five stars is the best rating)
loop (line 15) a metal ring used for hanging
aluminium (line 19) a light, silver-coloured metal
Teflon (line 19) a non-stick material used for cookware
enamel (line 20) enamel is a hard material used to decorate or
    protect metal, glass or similar materials
bamboo (line 22) a tropical plant with thick, hollow stems
SilverStone (line 27) a non-stick material used for cookware
hob (line 28) a surface on top of a cooker which can be heated;
    usually by gas or electricity
accessories (line 28) equipment or additional articles added to a
    product

LANGUAGE PRACTICE

A Put in the missing words. You can find all the words in the text. The first letters of the missing words are given.

   1 It is easy to use and gave good r____.
   2 The product had good quality ac____.
   3 The lid is en____.
   4 The pan is quite f__ and weak.
   5 You won't burn yourself; the handle is heat-r____.
   6 It gives the best performance and v__ for money.

B Answer the following questions. The answers to the questions all contain a specialist word or phrase. All the words appear in the text.

   1 What is the word for wooden or ivory utensils used for eating Chinese or Japanese food?
   2 What is the word for a light, silver-coloured metal?
   3 What is the word for a bowl-shaped dish used for frying food?
   4 What is the word for a tropical plant with thick, hollow stems? It can be used to make tables or chairs.

C Write a brief description of a wok (about 30 words) for a visitor to our planet who has never seen one before.

---

22 DATING

DATING
how to make the couple's connection

10 THINGS GIRLS DO THAT DRIVE GUYS CRAZY

We're talking drive-'em up-the-wall crazy. Here's the recipe for disaster:

1 Change your mind about how you feel toward him. Monday he's the guy of your dreams. Wednesday you've decided the new guy in your algebra class is the guy for you. By Friday, you've forgotten Mr Monday's name.

2 Compare yourself to other girls. If a guy is interested in you, he's not going to want to listen to you complain about how popular your best friend is or how pretty your sister is.

3 Base your opinions on what he thinks. He wants to know your views on something. Before you respond, you try to find out what he thinks.

4 Forget about plans you've made with him. If you make plans to see him or call him at a specific time, don't drop the ball.

5 Sell yourself short. When he congratulates you on a job well done, you brush it off as no big deal or give the credit to others.

6 Obsess about your weight. He orders a mega-burger with fries and a chocolate milk-shake. While picking at your green salad, no dressing, you talk about fat grams and lament about how you really want to lose weight.

7 Play dumb. There's behaviour that qualifies as dumb and then there's behaviour that qualifies as dumber. Guess which category this stunt falls into?

8 Leave all the decision-making about dates up to him. He's tapped out for ideas. Your brilliant suggestion? 'I don't know.' Hello! Wake up and read the paper! Check out the movie listings and offer an idea or two.

9 Act rude toward others. Walking all over other people in an attempt to impress him isn't going to score you any points.

10 Refuse to laugh at yourself. Your mom decides to show him some of your baby photos and you respond by stomping out of the living room in a huff? The ability to laugh at yourself shows that you've got confidence which is one of the most attractive qualities around. So, get some confidence . . . he'll be crazy about you!

(from *Teen Magazine*, May 1995)

GLOSSARY

dating (heading) to go out with someone. (Mainly American English)

guys (line 3) an informal word meaning men, more common in American English

drive crazy (line 3) make (someone) extremely annoyed

drive up the wall (line 4) to make somebody angry and frustrated

recipe for disaster (line 5) likely to result in disaster

drop the ball (line 18) to do something accidentally but which causes problems for yourself and others

sell yourself short (line 19) to show yourself as unimportant or unattractive

brush it off (line 20) to refuse to consider something or someone seriously

big deal (line 20) something impressive or important

mega-burger (line 22) a very large hamburger

fries (line 23) fried potatoes

picking at (line 23) to eat small amounts of food

dressing (line 24) a liquid made from oils and vinegar or lemon juice which is normally poured over salads

lament (line 25) to complain in a very sad way

dumb (line 26) stupid or silly (American English)

stunt (line 28) a stunt is a dangerous or, here, very stupid action

tapped out for ideas (line 30) to have no ideas at all

walk all over people (line 33) to be rude to or critical of other people

mom (line 35) mother or mum (American English)

stomping (line 37) to walk with very heavy steps, usually in anger or disappointment

in a huff (line 37) in an angry mood

crazy about (line 40) to be in love with

LANGUAGE PRACTICE

A Put in the missing words. You can find all the words in the text. The first letters of the missing words are given.

1 If you behave like that it is a recipe for d____.
2 If you make plans to see a friend at a sp____ time, don't drop the ball.
3 If you show yourself in a way which makes others believe you are not worth much, you s____ yourself sh____.
4 If you are obsessed about your weight, you will l____ about how you want to lose weight.
5 If you w____ over other people, you won't impress anybody.
6 Confidence is a very attractive qu____.

B   Answer the following questions. The answers to the questions all contain a specialist word or phrase. All the words appear in the text.

1 What is another word for man in American English?
2 What is another word for stupid or silly in American English?
3 What is another word for cinema film in American English?
4 What is another word for mother or mum in American English?

C   Write a brief description (approximately 50 words) of the most perfect person you would like to date.

_____

23   BEAUTY TIPS

1   10 TRIED AND TRUE BEAUTY TIPS

We've got your number: 10 great tips that'll help you look great.

1. Don't be flat! To give fine hair a boost, place your fingers on your scalp and rub in a circular motion as you blowdry your hair.

2. To stop eyeshadow from creasing, press a powder paper (ask for them at the beauty supply store) over your lids before you put on your eyeshadow.

3. Has styling product build-up gunked up your combs and brushes? Just sudsing with water may not get them clean. What works: A soaking in three parts water to one part bleach.

4. Want to find a great hair salon? The best way . . . word of mouth! So, before you make an appointment, ask friends with styles you like who does their hair.

5. Fir eye openers, forget thick, heavy eyeline. This'll make your eyes look small. Your best bet? Using an eyepencil, draw a fine line close to your lashes, then smudge it slightly using a cotton swab.

6. Read the labels! When choosing a shampoo, don't just grab one and suds up. As well as the hair type, take note of any special features such as being specially formulated for limp, chemically treated or damaged hair.

7. Is your lip pencil too hard? Dip it in a little lip balm. This will help soften it up, so it'll be easier to apply.

8. Tweezing your eyebrows at the last minute? Try using a cotton swab dampened with Visine to help take away any redness.

9. Say ahhhhhh! Opening your mouth and raising your eyebrows when you apply mascara helps to keep mascara off your eyelids.

10. Give your nails extra strength by using a hand cream on a regular basis. This stops moisture loss – one of the biggest causes of brittle and broken nails.

(from *Teen Magazine*, May 1995)

GLOSSARY

tip (heading) useful piece of advice or information

we've got your number (line 2) we know all about you

give a boost (line 4) to improve

scalp (line 5) the skin under the hair on your head

blowdry (line 6) to dry hair by blowing warm air through a hair drier

creasing (line 7) to make thin fine lines

eyeshadow (line 7) a substance of different colours which you can paint on your eyelids

gunked up (line 10) made sticky with thick liquid

suds (line 11) soap and water

bleach (line 13) a chemical substance used to clean things or make them white

hair salon (line 14) the place where your hair is cut and styled

word of mouth (line 15) information your friends tell you

fir (line 17) to get thicker

smudge (line 19) to make something wet and to spread it, ink or lipstick, etc

swab (line 20) a small piece of cloth or cotton wool which is used for cleaning something

specially formulated (line 23) made for a particular purpose

limp (line 24) soft, not stiff or firm

chemically treated (line 24) given special properties by means of chemicals

lip balm (line 25) an ointment which stops lips from being sore

tweezing (line 27) a pair of tweezers is a small tool used for picking up small objects or for pulling out hair

Visine (line 28) a commercial cleaning product

mascara (line 31) a substance to put on eyelashes to make them look darker and thicker

moisture (line 34) tiny drops of water. If there is moisture loss (for example from skin) it can become very dry

brittle (line 35) something which breaks easily

LANGUAGE PRACTICE

A Put in the missing words. You can find all the words in the text. The first letters of the missing words are given.

1 Here are some t____ that will help you look and feel better.
2 There is no need to advertise; people seem to hear about the restaurant by w____ of m____.
3 If you decide to go to the party, it will give everyone a b____.
4 A new hairdressing s____ has opened next to the supermarket.
5 Do you wear m____ on your eyelashes?
6 When choosing a shampoo, take note of any special f____ on the label.

B Answer the following questions. The answers to the questions all contain a specialist word or phrase. All the words appear in the text.

1 What is the word for the substance which you can paint on or apply to your eyelids?
2 What is the ointment which stops lips from being sore?
3 What is the word used for drying hair with a hair-drier?
4 What is put on eyelashes to make them look darker and thicker?

C With a partner who has read the text discuss whether you feel men should wear make-up. Give two reasons why they should or why they should not.

24 PROBLEM PAGES

A

Help when you need it ... our agony aunt Sue Frost
answers your letters.

Last week my best friend's mum died from cancer. We've always
5 been close – right through school and getting married – but now I
feel I'm letting her down. I don't know what to say without
sounding condescending or awkward. I want to phone or visit my
friend, but my husband says I'll be intruding on her grief and that
she'll come to me if she needs to. Please help – I lie awake at
10 night wondering what to say to comfort her. I feel so useless.

Everyone does when they're confronted with suffering and
death. There is no magic formula to make everything right
again. But that doesn't mean you can't do anything. A
hug, a kiss and just listening can all be really helpful at
15 times like these. The worst thing is to pretend that nothing
has happened and to ignore her grief because you're embar-
rassed or confused. So pick up that phone and let her know
you're thinking of her. It doesn't matter what you say –
just show that you care.

(from *Woman* magazine, August 1994)

B

1 STOP BOYFRIEND WOES

At first, you thought his small acts of jealousy were kind of cute.
He must really care, you thought, as he turned three shades of
green watching you wave across the hall to one of your ex-boy-
5 friends. How endearing, you mused, as he shyly asked you to
please stop seeing so much of your male friends. But now his

octopus act of keeping you at arm's distance from every other guy at school is getting old. How to get him to loosen his grip?

First, reassure him that you care for him and that you're not interested in seeing other guys. Then, tell him that his jealousy is making you feel trapped. Hopefully, this will make him back off. But, be prepared to give him a few reminders that you need some space, as possessiveness actually can't be cured overnight!

(from *Teen Magazine*, April 1994)

GLOSSARY

A

agony aunt (line 3) a person who writes for a newspaper or magazine and gives advice to readers about their personal problems

cancer (line 4) a very serious disease in which the cells in your body expand too quickly

let down (line 6) to let somebody down is to disappoint them

condescending (line 7) to treat somebody as if they were inferior

intrude (line 8) to disturb someone who wants to be quiet

magic formula (line 12) a way of doing something that will be immediately successful

B

woe(s) (line 1) problem; personal difficulty

kind of (line 2) an informal phrase meaning 'rather'

cute (line 2) a word which means 'attractive'; more frequent in American than British English

three shades of green (lines 3–4) different colours of green, meaning that you experience different feelings of envy

green (line 4) envious, jealous

ex-boyfriend (lines 4–5) someone who used to be your boyfriend

endearing (line 5) someone who is pleasant and likeable

mused (line 5) thought (formal word)

octopus act (line 7) to behave like an octopus; here to hold someone very tightly

possessiveness (line 13) wanting all the love and attention of
another person

LANGUAGE PRACTICE

A Put in the missing words. You can find all the words in the
text. The first letters of the missing words are given.

1 I know this will disappoint you so I am sorry to have
to l____ you d____.

2 He's so con____; he always tries to sound superior.

3 If you have a problem you can always write to the
a____ aunt.

4 David has just bought a new car and we're g____ with
envy.

5 If people are too possessive, you can feel tr____.

6 He's not my boyfriend anymore; he's an e____-____.

B Substitute the underlined words with a word or words
from the text. Make any grammatical changes which are
necessary.

1 I lie awake at night and wonder what to say which
will comfort her.

2 Everyone feels useless when they face suffering and
death.

3 The worst thing is a pretence that nothing has
happened.

4 You have no interest in seeing other guys.

C With a partner who has read the two texts write a letter
(about 30–40 words) to an agony aunt. One of you should
write the letter about a problem in your life; the other
should write a reply (about 30–40 words).

AMERICAN TOPICS   1

A Doctor at 17, He Next Hopes To Be a Nobel Prize Winner

Balamurali Ambati graduated last week from the Mount Sinai School of Medicine in New York at the age of 17.   5

'He certainly is among the youngest ever graduated from a U.S. medical school,' said Patty Shea of the Association of American Medical Colleges. She could not say if he was the youngest.

Dr Ambati, a native of Vellore, India, moved to Buf-   10
falo, New York, with his family when he was 3. His father is an industrial engineer and his mother is a math teacher. He was doing calculus at 4. At 11, he graduated from high school and co-authored a research book on AIDS with his older brother Jaya, who is now 24 and also a doctor. At 13,   15
he graduated from New York University.

He plays chess, basketball and ping pong and is just learning to drive. 'I was never called a nerd or geek or anything like that,' he said. Patients he has seen so far also don't seem to mind his age.   20

'Part of the reason, I think, is that I'm 6 feet tall, so most people can't readily tell I'm so young,' he said.

'But I have to say that once they learned about it through the grapevine, they tended to be very friendly and open-minded about it.'   25

Dr Ambati, who lives in the New York borough of Queens, will soon begin four years as an intern. He plans to specialize in ophthalmology. He says his next goal is the Nobel prize.

(from *The International Herald Tribune*, 20/21 May 1995)

GLOSSARY

Nobel prize (line 2) international prizes in various subjects awarded every year and begun by Alfred Nobel, the Swedish chemist and engineer

math (line 12) mathematics (abbreviation); ('maths', British English)

calculus (line 13) a particular method of calculating in mathematics

AIDS (line 14) Acquired Immune Deficiency Syndrome (abbreviation); an illness which destroys the body's natural system of protection against disease

ping pong (line 17) table tennis (informal)

nerd (line 18) a brainy person who is not liked and who is believed to be a fool (American English) (slang)

geek (line 18) someone who is ugly and spotty (American English) (slang)

through the grapevine (line 24) when news is passed from one person to another in casual conversation

open-minded (line 25) if someone is open-minded, they are willing to listen to different ideas and points of view

borough (line 26) a district, a part of a town or community

intern (line 27) a recent graduate living in a hospital and acting as an assistant doctor

ophthalmology (line 28) the scientific study of the eye

LANGUAGE PRACTICE

A Put in the missing words. You can find all the words in the text. The first letters of the missing words are given.

1 He gr___ recently from university.
2 He is a n___ of a small town called Vellore.
3 I heard through the gr___ that he is much younger than he looks.
4 My favourite sports are chess and p___ p___.
5 She is willing to listen to others and is always op___ -m___ about everything.
6 He wrote a lot with his brother. They co-___ a research book.

B Answer the following questions. The answers to the questions all contain a specialist word or phrase. All the words appear in the text.

1 What is the word for maths in American English?
2 What is the word for scientific study of the eye?
3 What is the word for an assistant doctor in a hospital, who has recently graduated?
4 What is the name for the annual international award given to people who have achieved a lot in their subject?

C Write a 50–75 word biography for yourself in which you list all the things you want to be or to achieve.

Technical Language

OPERATING INSTRUCTIONS

OIL CHARACTERISTICS

Multigrade oils to VW Standard 501 01 are reasonably priced oils with the following properties:
– All year round use in temperate climate areas.
– Excellent cleaning capability.
– Efficient lubrication at all engine temperatures and load conditions.
– High resistance to ageing.

The improved lubricity oils as per VW Specification 500 00 have in addition the following advantages:
– All year round use at practically all temperatures.
– Low frictional losses in the engine.
– Best possible starting even at very low temperatures.

Single grade oils. Due to their limited viscosity ranges these oils are not generally acceptable for all year round use.

In the case of petrol and turbocharged Diesel engines these oils should only be used if unavoidable – see previous page.

For the NA Diesel engine (not turbocharged) this oil can be economical, in the case of high annual mileage and provided that oil changes are carried out frequently.

When using SAE 10 W single grade oil or SAE 5 W–30 multi-grade oil, continuous high engine speeds and engine loading should be avoided.

This restriction does not apply when using improved lubricity oils.

(from a Volkswagen car handbook, 1995)

GLOSSARY

characteristics (line 2) what something is like

multigrade (line 3) good enough for many different uses

VW (line 3) Volkswagen, a German car (abbreviation)

temperate (line 5) a climate with weather that is never extremely hot or extremely cold

lubrication (line 7) the smoothing effect of oil

improved lubricity (line 10) having better smoothing quality

specification (line 10) the description, often in the form of a list, of the qualities of something

practically (line 12) almost

viscosity (line 15) thick and sticky, not flowing easily

turbocharged (line 18) an engine fitted with a fan to improve its performance

diesel (line 18) an engine in which a mixture of air and oil burns by pressure not electricity

SAE (line 24) a measure of oil thickness. SAE 10 W is a very thin oil

engine loading (line 26) using the engine with high power

restriction (line 27) something you cannot or should not do

LANGUAGE PRACTICE

A Put in the missing words. You can find all the words in the text. The first letters of the missing words are given.

1 VW Standard 501 oils are m____ and suitable for year round use.

2 They may not be appropriate in very hot or cold places, but are suitable in t____ c____ areas.

3 VW 500 00 oils avoid engine parts rubbing together, giving low f____ losses.

4 In cold weather, these oils permit good starting at very low t____.

5 Petrol and turbocharged Diesel engines should not use single grade oils unless this is un____.

6 With some oils, you should avoid high engine speeds, but this r____ does not apply to improved lubricity oils.

B Substitute the underlined words with a word or words from the text. Make any grammatical changes which are necessary.

1 501 are <u>quite cheap</u> oils.
2 VW Specification 500 00 oils <u>are also better for these reasons</u>.
3 Single grade oils are <u>usually wrong</u> for year round use.
4 <u>If you do a lot of driving</u>, this oil can offer you a saving.

C The handbook lists three advantages of VW Specification 500 00 oils over VW Standard 501. List at least three more advantages they have over single grade oils, but in the form of full sentences. You may wish to begin 'They are better because . . .'

27 FLYMO GUARANTEE: INFORMATION SHEET

SPECIAL FLYMO 3 YEAR *ALL* PARTS GUARANTEE

ON YOUR FLYMO GARDENVAC

1 All you need to do!
Simply complete the attached Flymo Registration Card and return to Flymo WITHIN 7 DAYS OF PURCHASE. Flymo will not acknowledge receipt but you will be automatically registered on the 3 Year Guarantee Scheme.

2 Your Flymo Cover
Once you have sent off your Registration Card your

Guarantee will cover *All Parts* for 3 years, under the terms set out in the back of the Operator's Manual. For the first 12 months period this cover also includes *Labour Costs* incurred in the repair of your GardenVac.

3 If your GardenVac needs repair . . .

15

Just take it to your nearest Authorised Flymo Service Repairer. For full details of Flymo's National Network of Service Repairers, see the Operator's Manual or the entries in Yellow Pages.

Your Service Repairer will require the following 20 information:

DATE OF PURCHASE _____

PRODUCT SERIAL NO _____

PURCHASED FROM _____

_____

NOTE: Please keep your proof of purchase as it will be needed when making a 25 claim under the guarantee.

(Flymo Guarantee for GardenVac, 1995)

GLOSSARY

Flymo (heading) a brand name of a manufacturer of lawnmowers
all parts guarantee (lines 1–2) the guarantee will cover the cost of any part which does not work
GardenVac (line 3) a piece of equipment for the garden that works in the same way as a vacuum cleaner
purchase (line 6) buy, buying
acknowledge (line 7) confirm that something has happened
cover (line 9) guarantee
labour costs (line 13) the costs of paying people to make repairs
incurred (line 13) neccesary
authorized (line 16) approved by the manufacturer
network (line 17) a widespread range of similar services
manual (line 18) a book of instructions

Yellow Pages (line 19) a phone book which gives telephone numbers for companies and businesses

serial no (line 23) a number used to identify one machine; 'no' is an abbreviation for 'number'

LANGUAGE PRACTICE

A Put in the missing words. You can find all the words in the text. The first letters of the missing words are given.

1 With your new machine, you must return the Registration Card within a week of pur____.

2 There's nothing else to do as you will be a____ registered.

3 In the back of the Operator's Manual, you will find the t____ of the guarantee.

4 Cover includes Labour Costs i____ in the first 12 months.

5 The Operator's Manual includes a list of the National N____ of Service Repairers.

6 To make a claim, you must demonstrate pr____ o____ pur____.

B Substitute the underlined words with a word or words from the text. Make any grammatical changes which are necessary.

1 The Guarantee will <u>apply to</u> all parts for three years.

2 For the <u>year</u>, Labour Costs are included.

3 Your Service Repairer will <u>need these details</u>.

4 <u>Name of supplier</u>.

C Is the GardenVac an essential gardening implement? Try and list all the garden implements you can think of, under two headings: Essential/Useful but not Essential.

28   INTERNAL FAX/MEMO

FROM: MARK TATCHELL–SMITH
ELECTRONICS
FAX (DIRECT) + 44–921–843424
TO: ALISON PAULUS
CC: DAN ELLIS
Subject: Computer Purchase

Hi! We're on our way to Caswell and I've stopped to fax
from the car. Just met Richard Haynes (MD at Wulfsons)
and agreed, as part of the re-fitting deal, that we'd supply
him with a laptop.   10

He wants at least 420 Mb of hard disk capacity and 16Mb
of RAM plus a power adaptor and portable printer. He
also wants an executive carrying case.

Could you call/fax/e-mail Kyle Barber and ask him for a
quote? Either Toshiba or Compaq. Fax back his quote.   15

Thanks a lot. Call my car if you don't understand.

P.S. Tell David. Good deal. Worth the laptop. More in the
pipeline.

(Smith Electronics fax, April 1995)

GLOSSARY

internal (heading) within the company only
memo (heading) memorandum (abbreviation), a message in which
   important things are recorded
CC (line 5) copies to be sent to . . . (abbreviation)
Hi! (line 7) A very informal greeting
MD (line 8) Managing Director (abbreviation), the head of a
   company
re-fitting (line 9) to buy new equipment or furniture
deal (line 9) business arrangement (informal)
laptop (line 10) a small portable computer

Mb (line 11) megabyte (abbreviation)

hard disk (line 11) the main disk fitted as part of the computer

RAM (line 12) random access memory (abbreviation). RAM only holds information when the computer is switched on

power adaptor (line 12) a machine which changes the strength of the electricity which powers the computer

executive (line 13) something that can be used by an important business person

e-mail (line 14) electronic mail sent between computers

quote (line 15) quotation (abbreviation), the price which will be charged

Toshiba/Compaq (line 15) brands of computer

in the pipeline (line 17) more of something will follow (idiomatic).

GRAMMAR AND STYLE NOTE

This fax is written in an informal style. Many faxes, like letters, are written much more formally, especially when they are for external communication. Here the sender and receiver know each other very well. The informal style here is created by vocabulary choices, especially abbreviations (for example, 'quote') but also by *ellipsis*. Ellipsis is a grammatical structure in which key grammatical words are left out. Examples of ellipsis are: 'Good deal' for 'It was a good deal'; 'Either Toshiba or Compaq' for 'It must be either Toshiba or Compaq'; 'Just met Richard Haynes' for 'I've just met Richard Haynes'. In formal letters it would not normally be appropriate to use ellipsis.

LANGUAGE PRACTICE

A Put in the missing words. You can find all the words in the text. The first letters of the missing words are given.

   1 As part of the d____, we will supply him with a l____.

   2 He wants an ex____ carrying case.

   3 Ask him to let us have a q____.

   4 I've stopped to f____ from the car.

   5 There will be more deals in the p____.

   6 The computer must have at least 420 Mb of h____ d____ capacity.

B What are the appropriate abbreviations for the following expressions? All the abbreviations are in the text.

   1 Copies to

   2 Memorandum

3 Quotation
4 Megabyte
5 Managing Director
6 Electronic Mail

C What do you think are the advantages and disadvantages of portable laptop computers? Write your answer in about 30–40 words.

---

29 MARROW (SOWING GUIDE)

MARROW (*Courgette*) *All Green Bush*   1
Use as a hot vegetable, excellent when fried, also in jam making.

QUICK GUIDE

	For Indoor Sowing	For Outdoor Sowing
WHEN	April to May	May
WHERE	In peat pots of moist compost	In a prepared seed bed
HOW	Sow 2 seeds per pot	Sow 2–3 seeds per position, 120 cm (48 in) between positions
	Cover with fine layer of compost	Cover lightly with fine soil
	Firm gently	Firm gently
	Cover with glass or polythene and shade with paper	Keep moist
	Keep at 15°C (60°F)	

CARE	Remove glass and paper when seedlings appear	Thin to one seedling per position
	Reduce to one plant per pot	Keep moist and weed free at all times
	At 5–6 leaf stage stand outside for a few days	Cut fruit regularly to promote further fruit development
	Transplant 120 cm (48 in) apart in June	
	Keep moist and weed free at all times	
	Cut fruit regularly to promote further fruit development	
HARVEST	July to September	July to September

TIP: When fruit start to swell a liquid feed every 7–10 days is recommended.

Performance subject to growing conditions

W W JOHNSON & SON LTD., LONDON ROAD, BOSTON, LINCS PE21 8AD, ENGLAND

EEC rules and standards. Standards seeds

(from a Johnson's Seeds packet)

GLOSSARY

marrow (heading) a vegetable. Courgette is another name for small marrows

sowing (heading) planting seeds in the ground

bush (line 1) a plant which is not very tall and quite wide

peat pots (line 7) pots made of peat, dead plant material found under the ground in cool, wet areas

moist (line 7) damp

compost (line 8) a mixture of dying plants and manure, added to the soil to help plants grow

polythene (line 16) transparent plastic

seedling (line 19) a very young plant

weed free (lines 22–23) without other harmful plants

transplant (line 27) plant again in a different place

liquid feed (line 35) food which is added like water to growing plants

subject to (line 37) depends on

EEC (line 40) European Economic Community. This group of nations is now known as the European Union (EU). It makes laws which all member countries must obey

LANGUAGE PRACTICE

A Put in the missing words. You can find all the words in the text. The first letters of the missing words are given.

1 Marrow is a good vegetable, e____ when fried.
2 The compost or soil should be pressed down gently, until it is f____.
3 Indoor plants, when they have five or six leaves, should stand outside at this s____.
4 Fruit will be fully grown between July and September, so this is the time to h____ it.
5 Growing plants, when the fruit starts to s____, should be given a liquid feed.
6 The seeds are s____ and meet EEC rules.

B Substitute the underlined words with a word or words from the text. Make any grammatical changes which are necessary.

1 In the pots, <u>spread compost thinly over the</u> seeds.
2 Cutting fruit regularly will <u>encourage the growth of the fruit</u>.
3 A <u>useful hint</u> is to feed swelling fruit.
4 Fruit production <u>depends upon</u> how plants are grown.

C Why do you think some people like growing their own vegetables? Give at least three reasons.

No fee is chargeable for this certificate

CERTIFICATE OF BIRTH

Name and Surname .... *Nicholas Harry James Brunner*

Sex .... *Male*

Date of Birth .... *Second December 1994*

Place ⎧ Registration   LEEDS
of   ⎨   District
Birth ⎩ Sub-district .... LEEDS

I, P. D. CHASE ....Registrar of Births and Deaths

for the sub-district of .... LEEDS ....in the

Registration District of............... LEEDS ....do hereby

certify that the above particulars have been compiled from an

entry in a register in my custody.

Date .. 22/12/94 ..   *P D Chase*

Registrar of Births and Deaths

CAUTION :— *It is an offence to falsify a certificate or to make or knowingly use a false certificate or a copy of a false certificate intending it to be accepted as genuine to the prejudice of any person, or to possess a certificate knowing it to be false without lawful authority.*

WARNING :— *This certificate is not evidence of the identity of the person presenting it.*

GLOSSARY

birth certificate (heading) an official document identifying a person by name, date, and place of birth

no fee is chargeable (line 1) there is nothing to pay

surname (line 3) the name you share with other members of your family. It is usually a last name

registration district (lines 6–7) area dealt with by the main regional office for record-keeping

sub-district (line 8) area dealt with by the local records office

registrar (line 9) a person whose job is to keep official records

hereby (line 11) with this document (a legal term)

compiled (line 12) made; put together

entry in a register (line 13) a record written into a book

custody (line 13) to be responsible for keeping something

caution (line 16) warning

knowingly (line 16) deliberately (to do something wrong)

genuine (line 17) true

identity (line 19) the name and appearance by which a person is known and recognized

LANGUAGE PRACTICE

A Put in the missing words. You can find all the words in the text. The first letters of the missing words are given.

  1 The certificate is free, so no fee is c____.
  2 Nicholas's birthday is December 2, his d____ o____ b____ is 1994.
  3 P D Chase is the R____ who keeps records of births and deaths.
  4 The Registration District is called Leeds, and so is the s____ -d____.
  5 False certificates are illegal, so a ca____ is included.
  6 The id____ of the person is not proved by this certificate.

B Substitute the underlined words with a word or words from the text. Make any grammatical changes which are necessary.

  1 I state with this document that I have a record of these particulars.
  2 It is illegal to make an untruthful certificate.

3 You must not copy a false certificate in order to use it to harm anybody.

4 The certificate <u>does not prove</u> that the person who presents it is the same person named on the certificate.

C 1 What are your two favourite names for a boy and for a girl? Can you say why? Do you like your own name?

2 The birth of a baby is sometimes called in English 'a happy event'. Write at least 50 words saying why this is not always a true description.

Food and Drink English

31   MENU: FAST FOOD RESTAURANT

Extra Value Meals

₁ Big Mac Meal	£2.88
McChicken Sandwich Meal	£2.88
Quarter Pounder Meal	£2.88

Flavour of the Month

₅ Megamac Meal	£3.69
Megamac	£2.28

Desserts

Hot Apple or Fruit Pie	67p
Donuts Five Varieties	52p
₁₀ Trifle	75p
Sundae (hot fudge, hot caramel, strawberry)	77p
Cone	20p
₁₅ Apple Pie and Ice Cream	£1.19

Salads

Chef Salad	Side Order	£1.49
	Main Course	£2.46
Garden Salad	Side Order	£1.23
₂₀	Main Course	£1.80

Sandwiches

Big Mac		£1.74
McChicken Sandwich		£1.74
Hamburger		49p
₂₅ Cheeseburger		59p
Filet–o–Fish	100% Pure Cod	£1.32

Chicken McNuggets

6 pieces	£1.49
9 pieces	£2.14
20 pieces	£4.23

₃₀

French Fries
Regular **57p**, Medium **85p**, Large £**1.05**

Breakfast

Big Breakfast	£1.29
Scrambled Eggs and English Muffin	**90p**
Bacon and Egg McMuffin	**99p**
Sausages and Egg McMuffin	**99p**
Pancakes and Sausage	£**1.29**
Hash Brown Potatoes	**52p**
English Muffin with Jam	**52p**

Beverages

Coca-Cola, Diet Coke, Sprite, Fanta	
Regular	**69p**
Medium	**79p**
Large	**89p**
Milk Shakes (*four flavours*)	**90p**
Milk	**45p**
Pure Orange Juice	**67p**
Natural Mineral Water	**49p**
Coffee	**60p**
Tea	**43p**
Hot Chocolate	**55p**

(Menu for McDonald's Restaurants, 1995)

GLOSSARY

Big Mac (line 2) a large McDonald's hamburger
McChicken (line 3) a McDonald's meal with chicken

Quarter Pounder (line 4) a hamburger with a weight of a quarter of a pound

Megamac (line 6) an extremely large hamburger

donut (line 10) a lump or ring of sweet dough cooked in hot fat; also spelled doughnut

trifle (line 11) a cold pudding made of layers of sponge cake, fruit, jelly, and custard

sundae (line 12) a dish of ice cream with cream and nuts or fruit on top

fudge (line 12) a sweet vanilla flavour

caramel (line 12) a flavour made with burnt sugar

strawberry (line 13) a fruit flavour

cone (line 14) a thin biscuit containing ice cream

side order (line 17) a small dish to accompany a main meal

cheeseburger (line 25) a hamburger with a slice of cheese

Filet-o-Fish (line 26) a McDonald's meal with fish

cod (line 26) a large white fish

Chicken McNuggets (line 27) a McDonald's meal with small pieces of fried chicken

French fries (line 31) the American name for potatoes which have been cut into strips and fried (chips; British English)

scrambled eggs (line 35) eggs which have been cooked in milk with a small piece of butter

muffin (line 35) a kind of small, round bread roll which you eat hot

Egg McMuffin (line 36) a McDonald's meal with fried egg and bacon and cheese in a muffin (see above)

pancakes (line 38) a fried dish made with milk and flour

hash brown potatoes (line 39) an American dish made with small pieces of potato

beverages (line 41) drinks (formal)

Coca-Cola/Diet Coke/Sprite/Fanta (line 42) trademarks of fizzy non-alcoholic drinks

milk shake (line 46) a cold drink of milk mixed with ice cream and a flavouring

LANGUAGE PRACTICE

A Put in the missing words. You can find all the words in the text. The first letters of the missing words are given.

1 The special offer this month is Megamac, the f____ of the month.
2 Different kinds of donut are available, in five v____.
3 You can have two different sizes of salad. The larger one is a complete m____ c____.
4 Fried potatoes are usually called chips in Britain, but F____ f____ is the usual term in the USA
5 In the morning, you can get such things as scrambled eggs and English muffin for b____.
6 Milk costs 45p, but flavoured m____ s____ cost twice as much.

B Substitute the underlined words with a word or words from the text. Make any grammatical changes which are necessary.

1 Big Mac, McChicken Sandwich and Quarter Pounder are good meals for the price.
2 If you don't want a salad meal, you can order a smaller salad dish to accompany another meal.
3 A wide range of drinks is available.
4 Coca-Cola and other drinks come in three sizes; small, medium, and large.

C List as many words as you can from the menu which are company trading names: for example, McChicken and McMuffin.

---

32 SANDWICH LOAF WRAPPER

SAINSBURY'S PREMIUM SANDWICH LOAF   1

Sainsbury's Premium Sandwich Loaf is made from premium quality flour and is given a longer bake to produce a characteristically superior quality loaf with a fuller flavour.

Approx. 24 Slices
The flour used to make your bread is produced by 'milling' (grinding) clean grains of wheat. Wheat is made up of three important parts:
Endosperm – 85% of wheat – the white part of wheat containing a mixture of starch and protein.
Bran – 12% of wheat – fibrous coat of wheat, an important source of dietary fibre, recognised for its value to a well balanced diet.
Wheatgerm – 3% of wheat – contains nutritious vitamins and oils

Different sorts of bread use different proportions of the parts of wheat. For instance white loaves are made only from white flour; brown loaves from a mixture of white flour and bran. Wholemeal, as the name implies, is made from all the parts of wheat.

Nutrition information

TYPICAL VALUES	PER 100 g (3.5 oz)	PER SLICE
ENERGY	233 k cal	71 k cal
	987 k J	303 k J
PROTEIN	8.6 g	2.6 g
CARBOHYDRATES	45.1 g	13.9 g
of which SUGARS	1.8 g	0.6 g
STARCH	43.3 g	13.3 g
FAT	2.0 g	0.6 g
of which SATURATES	0.9 g,	0.3 g
FIBRE	2.3 g	0.7 g
SODIUM	0.5 g	0.2 g
PER SLICE	71 CALORIES	0.6 g FAT

SAFETY FIRST: TO AVOID SUFFOCATION, KEEP THIS WRAPPER AWAY FROM CHILDREN

White Bread 800 gram

Flour used: Unbleached Untreated White Flour: Improver
added during mixing to enhance product quality.
Produced in the UK for J Sainsbury-plc Stamford Street, 40
London SEI 9LL

Ingredients
UNBLEACHED UNTREATED WHITE FLOUR, WATER, YEAST,
VEGETABLE FAT, SALT, SOYA FLOUR, VINEGAR, EMULSIFI-
ERS: MONO- AND DIGLYCERIDES OF FATTY ACIDS, 45
MONO- AND DIACETYLTARTARIC ACID ESTERS OF
MONO-AND DIGLYCERIDES OF FATTY ACIDS; FLOUR IM-
PROVER: L-ASCORBIC ACID (VITAMIN C)

For best before date see bag closure.
If freezing place in deep freeze on day of purchase, use 50
within 3 months.
Store in a cool dry place.

(from Sainsbury's loaf wrapper, 1995)

GLOSSARY

premium (line 1) best quality
characteristically (line 4) distinctly
grinding (line 7) crushing
starch and protein (line 10) solid, energy-giving parts of food
fibrous/fibre (lines 11 and 12) parts of food which aid digestion
nutritious vitamins (line 14) health-giving parts of food
proportions (line 16) shares
nutrition information (line 21) details of the content of food
g (line 23) grams (abbreviation), a unit of weight
oz (line 23) ounces (abbreviation), a unit of weight
k cal (line 24) kilo calories (abbreviation), a unit of measurement
    for the energy value of food
k J (line 25) kilo joules (abbreviation), a unit of energy or work
carbohydrates (line 27) parts of food which fill you up (and can
    make you put on weight!)
saturates (line 31) a type of fat

sodium (line 33) a chemical which is essential for health

suffocation (line 35) to be unable to breathe

unbleached (line 38) not made white

enhance (line 39) improve

ingredients (line 42) what something is made from

yeast (line 43) a product used in baking to lighten and raise the mixture

soya (line 44) a kind of bean

emulsifiers (lines 44–5) chemicals used to make the mixture more solid and to make it last longer

best before date (line 49) a date on the packaging which shows when the product should be eaten

bag closure (line 49) the tie which closes the bag

deep freeze (line 50) a very cold refrigerator

LANGUAGE PRACTICE

A Put in the missing words. You can find all the words in the text. The first letters of the missing words are given.

1 Baking longer produces better flavour and a c____ superior loaf.

2 Grains of wheat are 85% endosperm, which provides nutritious s____ and p____.

3 Good eating habits include bran as part of a w____ b____ d____.

4 Bread made from all parts of the wheat is called wh____.

5 One sl____ of this loaf contains 71 calories.

6 Eat within three months if you put the loaf in a d____ fr____.

B Substitute the underlined words with a word or words from the text. Make any grammatical changes which are necessary.

1 Different types of bread use <u>varying percentages</u> of endosperm, bran and wheatgerm.

2 <u>Do not give this bag to</u> children.

3   L-Ascorbic acid is the <u>name of what is put in</u> during mixing to make an improved loaf.
4   See the bag closure for the date <u>when you should eat this bread</u>.

C   1   Who do you think would be interested in the 'Nutrition Information' and the list of 'Ingredients'?
    2   Sainsbury's is a leading chain of British supermarkets. Try and give at least three reasons <u>for</u> and three reasons <u>against</u> shopping at supermarkets rather than at specialists' food shops such as bakers, butchers, greengrocers, etc.

---

33   SOFT DRINK CAN

diet Coke
REGISTERED TRADE MARK
diet Coca-Cola

low calorie soft drink with vegetable extracts
Ingredients: carbonated water, colour (caramel), artificial sweet- 5
ener (Aspartame), Phosphoric Acid, flavourings, citric acid, pre-
servative (E211), caffeine. Contains Phenylalanine
Can help slimming or weight control only as part of a calorie
controlled diet

Nutrition Information per 100 ml   10
ENERGY: 1.9kj, 0.4 kcal
PROTEIN: 0 g
CARBOHYDRATE: 0 g
FAT: 0 g

*NutraSweet and the NutraSweet symbol are registered   15
trade marks of the NutraSweet Company

BEST SERVED – ICE COLD
BEST BEFORE END – see base of can for date
CANNED UNDER AUTHORITY OF THE COCA-
20 COLA COMPANY BY THE COCA-COLA EXPORT
CORP IN THE UK AT LONDON W6 9HQ
Freephone consumer information 0800 227711 service available in UK mainland only
330 ml
25 ALU Please recycle
'diet Coke' and 'diet Coca-Cola' are registered trade marks
of The Coca-Cola Company

(from a Coca-Cola soft drink can, 1995)

GLOSSARY

diet Coke (line 1) a low calorie form of Coca-Cola
registered trade mark (line 2) the legal protected name or design
    of a product
calorie (line 4) a unit of measurement for the energy value of
    food
soft drink (line 4) drink containing no alcohol
extracts (line 4) substance which is made by a chemical process
carbonated (line 5) with added gas
preservative (line 6) a chemical added to food and drink to make
    them last longer
caffeine (line 7) a drug which occurs naturally in coffee
ml (line 10) millilitres (abbreviation)
NutraSweet (line 15) a low calorie sweetener
canned (line 17) placed in a can (metal container)
corp (line 21) corporation (abbreviation), a large company
freephone (line 22) a telephone service which you don't have to
    pay for
consumer (line 22) user
UK mainland (line 23) England, Wales, and Scotland, not includ-
    ing smaller islands or Ireland
ALU (line 25) made of aluminium, which can be recycled or
    used again

A Put in the missing words. You can find all the words in the text. The first letters of the missing words are given.

    1 The name 'diet Coke' is the reg____ tr____ m____ of this drink.

    2 The drink will help to keep your weight down only as part of a c____ c____ di____.

    3 It contains zero grams of f____.

    4 I____ c____ is the best temperature for serving.

    5 There is no charge for consumer calls to F____ 0800 227711.

    6 The aluminium in this can may be used again, so please re____.

B Substitute the underlined words with a word or words from the text. Make any grammatical changes which are necessary.

    1 The <u>sugar substitute</u> Aspertame is one of the ingredients.

    2 On the bottom of the can, you will find <u>the date by which the drink should be consumed</u>.

    3 The Coca-Cola Export Corp, UK, has canned this drink <u>with the approval</u> of the Coca-Cola Company.

    4 The Freephone service <u>does not apply outside Great Britain (England, Scotland and Wales)</u>.

C   1 Coca-Cola is an American product which is sold throughout the world. Try and give at least three reasons why you think this has happened.

    2 The can requests the consumer to recycle the aluminium. List as many other items you can think of which can be recycled, and write one sentence saying why recycling is desirable.

34 WINE LABEL

MARLBOROUGH SAUVIGNON BLANC

Montana: Montana is New Zealand's leading winemaker, and is the country's largest exporter of quality bottled wine. Sound viticultural development and winemaking techniques have earned Montana an international reputation for producing wines of both consistency and high quality.

Marlborough Sauvignon Blanc: Montana pioneered the development of Marlborough as a wine growing region and it is to the Sauvignon Blanc grape that the area owes much for its international fame.

Montana Marlborough Sauvignon Blanc is produced from grapes harvested from our Brancott state vineyard in April. The resulting wine is a straw colour with green tints, has a distinctive gooseberry fruit nose and a full, fruity palate balanced by clean, crisp acidity and a dry finish.

NEW ZEALAND
Marlborough
UK Importer, the House of Seagram, 17 Hartfield Road, London SW19 3SE

(from a House of Seagram wine label)

GLOSSARY

Sauvignon Blanc (line 1) a variety of grape used in making white wine

viticultural (line 4) relating to the growing of grapes for winemaking

consistency (line 6) reliability

pioneered (line 7) the first to do something

vineyard (line 12) fields where grapes are grown

straw colour (line 13) the colour of dry grass (yellow)

tints (line 14) suggestions of colour
distinctive (line 14) easily recognized
gooseberry (line 14) a green fruit with a rather sour taste
nose (line 14) the odour or perfume of wine
palate (line 15) taste
crisp (line 15) slightly bitter
acidity (line 15) the acid quality of the wine
finish (line 16) the taste after the wine is swallowed
House of (line 19) company

LANGUAGE PRACTICE

A Put in the missing words. You can find all the words in the text. The first letters of the missing words are given.

1 Montana exports more qu____ b____ wine than any other New Zealand winemaker.
2 Good practice has led to Montana's international rep____.
3 Marlborough vineyards were developed by Montana, who p____ wine growing in this area.
4 April is the month when Sauvignon Blanc grapes are ha____ in Brancott state.
5 The wine is yellow like s____ with green t____.
6 It can be easily identified by its d____ gooseberry fruit nose.

B Substitute the underlined words with a word or words from the text. Make any grammatical changes which are necessary.

1 New Zealand winemaker Montana sends more overseas from the country than any other company.
2 Montana produces wine which you can rely on.
3 Marlborough must be very grateful to the Sauvignon Blanc grape.
4 The wine has the smell of gooseberries and a fruity flavour. After drinking, the taste is not sugary.

C   1   When do you think it is appropriate to drink wine, and when is it not appropriate?
    2   Try and write three sentences which describe this wine in terms of a) colour, b) nose, c) palate and finish. Refer to the last sentence of the description, but use as few of the same words as you can.

---

35 RECIPE FOR CHOCOLATE BANANA PUDDING

1   CHOCOLATE BANANA PUDDING

Serves 6
Time to prepare: 15 mins
Time to cook: 40 mins
5 **Cals per portion: 225**

2oz (60g) margarine
2oz (60g) caster sugar
2 eggs, beaten
1 medium-size banana, mashed
10 *3½ oz (105g) white self-raising flour*
½ oz (15g) unsweetened cocoa powder

Custard:
2tbsp (30ml) custard powder
½ pt (300ml) skimmed milk
15 *1tbsp (15ml) sugar*

1   Use 1tbsp (15ml) of margarine to lightly grease six dariole or castle-pudding moulds. Cream the remainder with the caster sugar until light and fluffy, then gradually beat in the eggs a little at a time. Mix in the mashed banana.

108

2   Sift together the flour and cocoa, then fold into the   20
creamed mixture using a large, metal spoon. Fold in sufficient warm water to give a soft, dropping consistency.
3   Divide the sponge mixture between the prepared
moulds. Cover with foil or greaseproof paper.
4   Transfer the pudding moulds to a steamer and steam   25
for 40 mins or until cooked through. Make sure the steamer
doesn't boil dry by topping up with boiling water from
time to time.
5   Make up custard with the skimmed milk and sugar according to the maker's instructions.   30
6   Carefully turn out the cooked puddings and serve with
the custard.

(from *Woman* magazine, August 1994)

GLOSSARY

cals (line 5) calories (abbreviation)
portion (line 5) amount of food for one person
margarine (line 6) a product like butter but made without milk
caster sugar (line 7) finely ground white sugar
mashed (line 9) squashed until it is like cream
self-raising flour (line 10) flour used in baking which helps to
    lighten and raise the mixture
cocoa (line 11) a powder, made from beans, which makes a choco-
    late flavour
custard (line 12) a sweet sauce, made from milk and eggs, to
    accompany puddings
tbsp (line 13) tablespoon (abbreviation)
pt (line 14) pint (abbreviation), 1 pint = 0.568 litre
skimmed milk (line 14) milk from which the fat has been
    removed
grease (line 16) provide a layer of fat, so the mixture does not
    stick to the container
moulds (line 17) a container for the pudding with a special shape
cream (line 17) to make smooth, like cream
sift (line 20) mix (applied to powders)

fold (line 20) mix gently

sufficient (lines 21–22) enough

consistency (line 22) the consistency of a food mixture is the degree to which it is thick and smooth

sponge (line 23) another name for this kind of pudding

foil (line 24) paper-thin sheets of metal

greaseproof paper (line 24) paper that does not go soft when touched by fat or steam

steamer (line 25) a pan which is placed over another pan of boiling water so that the food is cooked by steam

boil dry (line 27) boil until all the water has gone

topping up (line 27) adding

make up (line 29) prepare

turn out (line 31) empty the contents out

LANGUAGE PRACTICE

A Put in the missing words. You can find all the words in the text. The first letters of the missing words are given.

1 The banana should be m____, not whole.

2 The milk for the custard should be sk____, with the fat removed.

3 At stage 2, a soft c____ should be achieved by adding warm water.

4 After stage 3, you should t____ the moulds to a steamer.

5 T____ u____ the steamer may be necessary, so it doesn't boil dry.

6 When everything is ready, t____ o____ the puddings from the moulds and add custard.

B Substitute the underlined words with a word or words from the text. Make any grammatical changes which are necessary.

1 Margarine can be used to spread a thin layer of oil in the moulds.

2 Add enough water to make the mixture soft.

3 Steam for 40 minutes or until <u>completely ready</u>.
4 When making custard, you should follow the <u>guidelines given by the manufacturer</u>.

C 1 Do you think you would enjoy Chocolate Banana Pudding? Try and say why or why not.
2 What is your favourite food? Can you tell someone else how to prepare it? If not, list at least four more of your favourite dishes, to make up a complete menu.

The Language of Information

36   FILM FEATURES

From Friday 12th August 1994 to Thursday 18th August 1994 inclusive

SIRENS   15
Artist Norman Lindsay is asked to remove a controversial picture from an art exhibition. When he refuses, Anthony Campion (Hugh Grant) visits him in an effort to persuade him to pull the picture. Campion's wife, along for the ride, undergoes a sexual awakening, thanks to house residents and models, Sheela (Elle MacPherson), Prue (Kat Fischer) and Gibby (Portia de Rossi). The film is set in the picturesque Blue Mountains of Australia in the 1930's.
5.10 7.30 9.35 11.40

MAVERICK   PG
Based on the American television series of the same name, this action comedy stars Mel Gibson in the role made famous by James Garner (who also stars in this version). The smooth-talking gambler finds himself in competition with the woman he loves (Jodie Foster) and his rival for her affections (Garner) in a high-stakes poker championship. Directed by Richard Donner ('Lethal Weapon').
11.30 2.00 4.35 7.10 9.45 12.15

STAGGERED   15
In this comedy adventure, a toy salesman is in a fight against time to arrive at his wedding on time. After a wild night on the town, the bridegroom finds himself on a Scottish Island, the brunt of a joke played on him by his best man. Getting over his hangover is only one of the many obstacles he must face. The film stars Martin Clunes, Griff Rhys-Jones and Anna Chancellor.
8.10 10.15 12.30

BEVERLY HILLBILLIES   PG
America's zaniest billionaires are back in this full-length
feature film based on the popular 1960's television series.
After discovering oil on their property, the down-home
Clampetts load up their truck and head to Beverly Hills,
land of swimming pools and movie stars. Jim Varney
plays Uncle Jed, with Cloris Leachman as Granny, Dabney
Coleman as Mr Drysdale and Lilly Tomlin as Miss
Hathaway.
4.25 7.00 9.20 11.20

GETTING EVEN WITH DAD   PG
Macauley Culkin and Ted Danson join forces in this contemporary comedy as a father and son whose relationship
has never been very good. Culkin plays Timmy, an 11
year old boy who blackmails his father to get him to toe
the line. A con-man and crook, Danson's character finds
himself forced to bond with his son after the kid hides the
loot from his latest scam.
11.50 2.25 4.45 7.00

THE FLINTSTONES   U
John Goodman plays the ever-loving caveman, Fred Flintstone, in this live-action version of the popular animated
television series from Hanna-Barbara. Elizabeth Perkins,
Rick Moranis and Rosie O'Donnell join him in the roles
of Wilma, Barney and Betty. Kyle MacLachlan and Halle
Berry join the fun as Fred's boss and the seductress secretary
he has hired.
12.10 12.40 2.20 3.00 4.30 5.15 7.15 7.35 9.25 9.50
11.30 12.00

SNOW WHITE & THE SEVEN DWARFS   U
Originally released more than half a century ago, 'Snow
White' was the very first full-length animated feature. This
landmark film has been reissued with a newly-restored
theatrical print. Adapted from the Grimm's Fairy Tale

₆₅ story, the Disney classic can only be seen at a movie theatre.

12.00 1.55 4.05 6.15

THE CROW   18
After he and his girlfriend are murdered, a young man
₇₀ returns from the grave in the form of a crow to avenge
their deaths. Based on the novel by James O'Barr, this
Gothic horror film stars the late Brandon Lee in his final
role. Directed by Alex Proyas.

8.00 10.10 12.25

₇₅ MY GIRL 2   PG
Anna Chlumsky returns to her highly acclaimed role as
Vada in the sequel to the 1991 family saga. Vada is growing
up, her father (Dan Ackroyd) realises after she falls in love
on a trip to California. Jamie Lee Curtis also returns.
₈₀ 11.55 2.10

FOUR WEDDINGS AND A FUNERAL   15
This romantic comedy tells the story of a group of friends
who are reunited at the social events related in the title.
The film focuses on Charles (Hugh Grant), a confirmed
₈₅ bachelor who unwittingly falls in love with Carrie (Andie
MacDowell).

11.40 2.05 4.40 7.20 10.00 12.20

(from *Showcase Cinemas Brochure*, 1994)

GLOSSARY

15 (line 3) a film people of 15 and over can see
PG (line 13) a film for children to see with their parents
poker (line 19) a card game played usually to win money
brunt (line 26) the main target or victim
hangover (line 27) a sick feeling produced by drinking too much
     alcohol

down-home (line 34) living in a simple and honest way
getting even (line 41) acting in revenge for something
con-man (line 46) a person who tricks others, usually for money
scam (line 48) a trick, usually to get money
seductress (line 56) a woman who uses her sex to get other men
U (line 60) a film everyone can see
Disney (line 65) the Walt Disney film studios
18 (line 68) a film people of 18 years and over only can see
Gothic horror (line 72) a style popular in the eighteenth–
    nineteenth centuries
confirmed bachelor (lines 84–85) a man who does not want to get
    married

GRAMMAR AND STYLE NOTE
In summaries of films or books the simple present tense is often used to describe the action.
This choice of tense involves the reader, making it seem as if the action is happening now
before our eyes. It makes you want to buy the book or see the film. See also the next unit
'TV page'.

LANGUAGE PRACTICE

A Put in the missing words. You can find all the words in the
 text. The first letters of the missing words are given.

1 Mel Gibson and James Garner compete for a lot of
 money in a h____-s____ poker championship.
2 The character Fred Flintstone is a c____ who lived in
 prehistoric times.
3 The film 'Snow White' was made over fifty years ago,
 so it is more than half a c____ old.
4 In 'The Crow' a man who has been killed returns to
 life as a crow, in order to punish the murderer. He
 wants to a____ the deaths of himself and his girlfriend.
5 Anna Chlumsky appears again in her successful role as
 Vada, for which she was highly a____ in 1991.
6 Without realizing what is happening Charles u____
 falls in love with Carrie.

B Substitute the underlined words with a word or words
 from the text. Make any grammatical changes which are
 necessary.

1 Campion's wife <u>accompanies him simply for the sake</u> <u>of making the trip</u>.

2 A seller of toys <u>has to hurry</u> to arrive <u>at the correct</u> <u>hour</u> for his wedding.

3 Culkin's character, Timmy, blackmails his father so that he is forced <u>to behave honestly</u>.

4 'The Crow' features the actor Brandon Lee, <u>who has</u> <u>now died</u>.

C 1 From the descriptions try and say (in 50 words) which film you think you would like best. Give at least three reasons.

2 What is the difference between
   —live–action/animated
   —full–length feature/television series?

37 TV PAGE

1   BBC1
   6.00   **Business Breakfast**
   7.00   **BBC Breakfast News**
   9.05   **Kilroy** Discussion
5 10.00 **News; Regional News; Weather**
   10.05 **Good Morning . . . With Anne and Nick** Anne Diamond and Nick Owen host the morning magazine.
   12.00 **News; Regional News; Weather**
10 12.05 **Pebble Mill** With Gloria Hunniford.
   12.55 **Regional News; Weather**
   1.00   **One O'Clock News; Weather**
   1.30   **Neighbours** Wayne's detective work pays dividends.
15 1.50   **The Great British Quiz** General knowledge quiz.

2.15 **Knots Landing**

3.00 **Movie Magic**

3.25 **Cartoon Triple Bill** 3.45 **Monster Cafe** 4.00 **The All New Popeye** 4.20 **Mortimer and Arabel** 4.35 **Mighty Max** 4.55 **Newsround** 5.10 **Blue Peter**

5.35 **Neighbours**

6.00 **Six O'Clock News; Weather**

6.30 **Regional News Magazine**

7.00 **Telly Addicts** Noel Edmonds hosts a competitive rummage through the TV archives.

7.30 **Watchdog** Live consumer magazine presented by Anne Robinson.

8.00 **EastEnders** Michelle takes Pauline on a girls' night out.

8.30 **Les Dawson:** The Entertainer. Michael Parkinson remembers some of the late comedian's funniest moments.

9.00 **Nine O'Clock News; Regional News; Weather**

9.30 **Panorama:** The Uneasy Peace. Fergal Keane reports on the troubled mood of Northern Ireland's Unionist community in the wake of the IRA ceasefire.

10.10 **Nice Day at the Office** Phil Bachelor reluctantly steps into his boss's shoes and stumbles into a titanic struggle for power, survival and a dozen beautiful women.

10.40 **Film 94 With Barry Norman** Reviews of Quentin Tarantino's Pulp Fiction, starring John Travolta; and crime thriller The Client.

11.10 **FILM: Cat On A Hot Tin Roof** Stars Elizabeth Taylor and Paul Newman. Film version of Tennessee Williams' steamy stageplay about the family of a dying patriarch, battling to secure the inheritance. (1958; see Critics' Choice, S)

12.45 **Snooker from Derby**

1.55–2.00 **Weather**
3.00–3.30 **BBC Select** RCN Nursing Update.

(from *The Observer*, 16 October 1994)

GLOSSARY

BBC 1 (line 1) the main TV channel of the British Broadcasting Corporation

morning magazine (lines 6–7) a programme with different parts like cooking, fashion, celebrity interviews

Pebble Mill (line 10) a studio in Birmingham where another 'magazine'-type programme is made

Neighbours (line 13) an Australian 'soap opera' (a TV drama serial about the daily lives and problems of a group of people)

pays dividends (lines 13–14) is successful. 'Dividends' is another word for 'profits'

Knots Landing (line 16) an American soap opera

rummage (line 26) to search through things in a hurry

archives (line 26) a collection of old things, usually papers, photographs, books, old films etc

consumer (line 27) a consumer is anyone who buys goods and services

EastEnders (line 29) a British soap opera, set in East London

Panorama (line 36) a documentary programme on current affairs

Unionist (line 38) Irish supporters of a Union with and within Great Britain

in the wake of (line 38) after, following

IRA (line 38) Irish Republican Army (abbreviation), a group fighting for an independent and united Northern and Southern Ireland

ceasefire (line 39) the end of gun battles in a war

Nice Day at the Office (line 40) a 'sitcom' (a situation comedy, which shows the characters in amusing situations similar to everyday life)

stumbles (line 41) to meet something or somebody unexpectedly

titanic (line 41) very big and important

steamy (line 49) erotic

patriarch (line 50) the father of a family (formal)

inheritance (line 50) money or property which you receive if someone dies
RCN (line 54) Royal College of Nursing (abbreviation)

LANGUAGE PRACTICE

A Put in the missing words. You can find all the words in the
   text. The first letters of the missing words are given.

   1 In 'Neighbours', Wayne's successful investigation
      p___s d___.
   2 At 7.00, Noel Edmonds shows some old film from the
      BBC ar___.
   3 The next programme is shown as it is being made.
      Anne Robinson hosts this l___ show.
   4 Since the IRA agreed to put down their weapons,
      Fergal Keane reports on Unionist reactions to the
      c___.
   5 The film at 11.10 shows a family in conflict over inher-
      itance when the p___ is dying.
   6 Frequent w___ forecasts are given, at 10, 12, 12.55, 1,
      6, 9, and 1.55.

B Substitute the underlined words with a word or words
   from the text. Make any grammatical changes which are
   necessary.

   1 The programme at 1.50 is a competition with ques-
      tions on many subjects.
   2 From 3.25 to 3.45, three cartoons will be shown.
   3 In 'Nice Day at the Office' Phil takes over from his
      boss.
   4 Barry Norman gives his opinions of 'Pulp Fiction' and
      'The Client'.

C 1 Make a list of at least *five* differences between this TV
      page and the Film Features immediately before. For
      example, which one makes it easier for you to decide
      what to watch?

2   If you had to make a schedule for a full day's television, to appeal to all possible tastes, what balance would you choose? Consider news/drama/documentary/comedy/children's programmes/quiz shows/movies/sport. How important is the time of day? Write a schedule (about 50 words) from 4.00–9.00 p.m. for a TV station in your country.

---

38   HOTEL INFORMATION

1   HOTEL INFORMATION

As Forte Hotels are noted for their traditional hospitality, we aim to provide a friendly personal service which is as welcome to those on business as it is for a leisure stay. We hope that you will find all your needs in the facilities listed below. However if you require a service that is not here, please ask at Reception and we will do our best to help you.

BABY LISTENING   A baby listening service is available, dial 0.

BABY SITTING   A baby sitter can be arranged with suitable prior notice. Please arrange in advance with Reception.

CARS   Should you wish to hire a car during your stay, or should your car require repairs, service or petrol contact Reception, who will make all the arrangements for you.

CHURCHES RELIGIOUS SERVICES   Please ask at Reception for details of places of worship and service times.

COMMENTS   We invite all comments which you may

have about our hotel; if you require the assistance of our Duty Manager in answering any of these we are always available to help in any way possible.

DEPARTURE   Check out time is normally 12.00 noon. ₂₅ Should you require your room for longer, Reception will make every effort to accommodate you.

DOCTOR/DENTIST/CHEMIST   Should you require any of these services, please contact Reception who will be able to provide names and telephone numbers. The accounts ₃₀ of any Doctor or Dentist you use should be settled direct.

DRY CLEANING & LAUNDRY SERVICE   The hotel provides a laundry and dry cleaning service, five days a week. The service normally takes a day so we do ask that if you require ₃₅ this service that the items are brought to Reception no later than 9.30 am.

EARLY MORNING CALLS   To book your early morning call please contact Reception or dial 0.

FIRE   For your safety, please familiarise yourself with the ₄₀ fire instructions in your room. In the event of an emergency, dial 0.

FLOWERS/FLORISTS   For flowers in your room, or to send, dial 0.

FORWARD BOOKING   To make a free onward reserva- ₄₅ tion at the Forte Hotel of your choice, simply dial 0. If you require any help with your next destination or further reservations our receptionist will be only too glad to assist.

HAIRDRYER   If you require the use of a hairdryer please ask at Reception or dial 0. ₅₀

IRON   An iron and ironing board are available for your use. Please dial 0.

LUGGAGE   For assistance with luggage, please dial 0.

MAIL   Your mail can be stamped by us at Reception. Last postal collection each day is 17.00, except on Saturday ₅₅ and Sundays 12.00 noon.

NEWSPAPERS   Please order the newspaper of your

choice from Reception and it will be delivered to your room.

60 NIGHT SERVICE We are unable to offer the services of a night porter. In case of an emergency the Duty Manager can be contacted by using the telephone on the Reception desk. If you are unable to leave your room please dial 9 336 3931.

65 PAYMENT OF ACCOUNTS Guests are required to settle their accounts on departure, unless prior arrangements have been made to forward your account to your company. Cheques are accepted up to the value of the accompanied cheque guarantee card. Eurocheques are also accepted, as

70 are Travellers Cheques supported by proof of identity. The following credit cards are also accepted: Forte Gold Card, Access/Master-Card, Visa, American Express and Diners Club.

PUBLIC PHONES There is a public phone in the Recep-

75 tion area of the hotel.

ROOM SERVICE Room service is available from 7.00 am–9.00 pm. Please dial 0.

SHOE SHINE A shoe cleaning machine is located on the first floor landing.

80 SHOP A selection of toiletries including razors and tights are available from Reception at normal retail prices.

TAXIS We are able to order a taxi for you. We recommend early reservation of taxis. Please dial 0.

VALUABLES The management cannot accept responsibil-

85 ity for guests' effects left on the premises, but a valuable item may be deposited for safekeeping against a receipt signed by the Manager or member of the Reception staff. The receipt must be retained as it will be required as the authority for the item to be withdrawn from deposit.

90 VENDING A cigarette vending machine is located in the Reception area of the hotel.

(from a Forte Hotels catalogue, 1994)

GLOSSARY

facilities (line 5) services and equipment which are provided

baby listening (line 9) someone listens for a child's crying through an intercom while the parents are out

baby sitting (line 11) someone stays with children to look after them while the parents are out

worship (line 19) the act of praying, normally in a church

accommodate (line 27) to help (formal)

account (line 30) the detailed record of a bill

dry cleaning (line 33) cleaning clothes with a liquid chemical rather than water

night porter (line 61) someone on duty at the Reception Desk of a hotel throughout the night

toiletries (line 80) things you use when cleaning your body (for example, soap, toothpaste, shampoo)

tights (line 80) clothing for the legs, usually made of light material which stretches

effects (line 85) property, things which belong to you (formal)

premises (line 85) the buildings and grounds

authority (line 89) permission

LANGUAGE PRACTICE

A Put in the missing words. You can find all the words in the text. The first letters of the missing words are given.

1 If you want to go to church, Reception can give details of places of w___.

2 If you need the telephone to wake you up, ask at Reception for an e___ m___ c___.

3 If you are moving on to another Forte Hotel, dial 0 for an o___ r___.

4 Unless you have made p___ a___, you must pay when you leave.

5 You must keep any receipt for valuables, as this will be r___ to get items back.

6 Cigarettes are available from a v___ m___ in the Reception area.

B   Substitute the underlined words with a word or words
    from the text. Make any grammatical changes which are
    necessary.

    1   We welcome any remarks about the hotel.
    2   You must pay any Doctor's or Dentist's bills directly.
    3   Reception can post your letters.
    4   Toiletries are sold in the hotel shop at the same prices
        as in other shops.

C   This information is for a mid-priced hotel. List as many
    facilities as you can which you would expect to find in a
    luxury hotel but which are not mentioned here. For exam-
    ple, there is no mention here of a bar or restaurant.

---

39   MILK MESSAGE

Dear Valued Customer

A MESSAGE FROM YOUR CO-OP MILKMAN
You are probably aware of some of the major changes
happening to the British Dairy Industry. I would like to
take the opportunity to explain the action CWS Milk
Group have taken to protect our service relationship with
you, despite the increases in the cost of milk to us from the
Milk Marketing Board (Milk Marque).
    On the 1st July 1994 there was a rise in the price of milk
charged to all dairies. Since this date we have held back on
any increase to you, our valued doorstep customer.
    Whilst we face still further increases in milk prices
charged to us, *we are at present only increasing our price by 1p
per pint. I hope that the action we have taken will give you
confidence to continue to support us during these difficult times
safeguarding our unique British service.*

The Co-op home delivery service performs a valuable social role within the community to all sectors, particularly to the aged, disabled and households with children. To all customers I offer on a daily basis a full range of milk types 20 and a very competitively priced range of essential food items.

Please find enclosed coupons worth £2.00, as a special thank you for your continued support.

YOUR FRIENDLY CO-OP MILKMAN 25
Effective date Sunday 30th October 1994

(from CWS Milk Group Message, October 1994)

GLOSSARY

milkman (line 2) a person who brings milk every day to people's homes

dairy (line 4) milk and milk-based products (for example, butter, cheese)

CWS (line 5) Co-operative Wholesale Society (abbreviation); a company which specializes in food sales

doorstep customer (line 11) customers who are served at their doors

safeguard (line 16) to protect

unique (line 16) very special

coupon (line 23) a piece of paper which allows you to pay less for something

effective date (line 26) the date on which something will start

LANGUAGE PRACTICE

A Put in the missing words. You can find all the words in the text. The first letters of the missing words are given.

  1 Co-op milk sales are affected by changes to the British D___ I___.

  2 The Milk Marketing Board has the new alternative name of Milk M___.

3   We have to pay more again, but a____ p____ you will pay only an extra 1p per pint.
4   The social role of our delivery service is valuable to the c____.
5   The food items I offer are not expensive. They are v____ c____ priced.
6   You can save £2.00 by using the enclosed c____.

B   Substitute the underlined words with a word or words from the text. Make any grammatical changes which are necessary.

1   CWS Milk Group have taken action to <u>retain your custom.</u>
2   Your continued confidence will help us to protect a <u>service which is only available in Britain.</u>
3   Since 1 July 1994, we have <u>delayed</u> putting up our prices.
4   <u>On 30 October 1994, the new prices will begin.</u>

C   1   In one sentence, what is the principal information that 'your Co-op' milkman is conveying?
    2   In approximately 20 words say why the fourth paragraph (lines 17–22) is different from the rest of the milkman's message.

---

40   WEATHER FORECAST

1   WEATHER
By the BBC's **Susanne Charlton**

All parts should have a little sunshine from time to time today, but there will be some showers. The showers will
5   fall from early morning on north-facing coasts and it will feel quite wintry over Scotland. By the end of the morning the showers will become more widespread in the north,

with some of them turning sharp. Southern England and
South Wales may stay dry with the rest of England and
Wales becoming largely dry by evening. It will be another
cool and breezy day everywhere.

SUMMARY: BREEZY, SUN AND SHOWERS

LONDON & SOUTH-EAST: Mainly dry and bright. Wind light to
moderate, max 11c 52f.

SOUTH: Showers, heavy at times, perhaps with hail or sleet. Wind
moderate, max 10c 50f.

SOUTH-WEST & CHANNEL ISLES: Showers and sunny periods.
Mainly dry later. Wind moderate, max 11c 52f.

MIDLANDS: Becoming dry after a sunny and showery start. Wind
moderate, max 11c 52f.

WALES: Showers, drying out later with some sun. Wind moderate, max 11c 52f.

EAST ANGLIA: Showers, drying out later with some sun. Wind
moderate, max 11c 51f.

NORTH EAST & YORKS: Becoming dry after a sunny and showery start. Wind moderate, max 11c 52f.

NORTH WEST: Showers, drying out later with some sun. Wind
moderate, max 11c 52f.

SCOTLAND: Sunny periods and wintry showers. Dry but cloudy
later. Wind light to moderate, max 9c 48f.

IRELAND: Sunny periods and showers, cloudy with rain later.
Wind moderate, max 10c 50f.

SEA: Channel and S North Sea: Wind N to NE moderate, visibility moderate. Irish Sea: Wind N to NW moderate, showers
dying out. Visibility good, sea slight.

(from *The Daily Mail*, 13 May 1995)

GLOSSARY

showers (line 4) short periods of light rain
breezy (line 11) with moderate wind
moderate (line 14) neither strong nor weak

c (line 14) degrees centigrade/celsius (abbreviation), a temperature scale with freezing point at 0°
f (line 14) degrees fahrenheit (abbreviation), a temperature scale
with freezing point at 32°
max (line 14) maximum temperature (abbreviation)
sunny periods (line 17) periods of sunshine, usually coming in between showers
visibility (lines 33–4) the distance you can see
slight (line 35) with small movements, not strong or rough

LANGUAGE PRACTICE

A Put in the missing words. You can find all the words in the
text. The first letters of the missing words are given.

1 Everywhere will be fine, with a little s____.
2 Later, most of the north will have rain, with showers
becoming w____.
3 It may not rain at all in the south, and, at the end of
the day, other parts of England and Wales will be
l____ dry.
4 Scotland will be cold with w____ showers.
5 Conditions at sea will be quite clear, with v____ better
in the Irish Sea than in the Channel.
6 Briefly, the s____ for today is Breezy.

B Substitute the underlined words with a word or words
from the text. Make any grammatical changes which are
necessary.

1 This forecast is by Susanne Charlton, who works for
the BBC.
2 The sun will shine occasionally today.
3 In London and the South-East the wind will not be
strong.
4 Showers in the South may be icy.

C 1 Write a brief paragraph (50 words maximum) saying why
you would enjoy or not enjoy a day like this in Wales.

2 Do you ever read or listen to weather forecasts? How reliable do you think they are? Would you ever change your plans if bad weather was forecast?

---

41 NATIONAL SCHOOL TESTS

NATIONAL TESTING AND ASSESSMENT IN SCHOOLS IN 1995

In 1995, all schoolchildren aged 7, 11 and 14 will take straightforward national tests in the basic subjects. 11 year-olds will be taking the national tests for the first time.

During the school year, teachers will also assess their pupils' work. These assessments will give you useful information about how your child has got on in English, mathematics and science in his or her school work. Set alongside the national test results, these 'teacher assessments' will give a clear picture of your child's overall achievements during the school year.

This leaflet explains what these National Curriculum tests will be like.

WHAT THE TESTS ARE FOR
The purpose of the tests is to find out what children have learned in the most important subjects by the key ages of 7, 11 and 14.

The test will enable teachers and parents to check whether children are reaching the national standards set out in the National Curriculum and to provide help where children fall short of national standards.

The tests will be used across England so parents will know how their children are doing compared with children of the same age.

In time, it will be possible to compare how the same children did in the tests at age 7, at age 11 and at age 14. This will help to show how much progress children have made over time.

30 It is not the purpose of the tests to enable secondary schools to decide which children to give places to.

WHAT THE TESTS ARE LIKE

All 7, 11 and 14 year-olds will have to take the tests in 1995.

35 The tests will concentrate on the basics

7 year-olds will be tested in reading, writing, spelling, handwriting and mathematics.

11 year-olds and 14 year-olds will be tested in English, mathematics and science.

40 The tests will show whether children have reached the National Curriculum learning targets that they have been aiming for in their school work.

(from Department for Education (DFE) leaflet, 1995)

GLOSSARY

straightforward (line 4) simple
National Curriculum (line 13) the subjects and the different courses of study which have to be taught in English schools
key (line 17) very important
secondary schools (lines 30–31) Schools for pupils between the ages of 11 or 12 and 18
target (line 41) something to aim at

LANGUAGE PRACTICE

A Put in the missing words. You can find all the missing words in the text. The first letters of the missing words are given.

1 Assessments of progress will show how your child has g___ o___.
2 Teachers and parents can provide help when children f___ s___ of national standards.
3 National tests will be used a___ England.
4 The tests will concentrate on b___ such as English, mathematics, and science.
5 The youngest children to take the tests will be 7 y___-o___.
6 Children have been a___ f___ National Curriculum learning targets.

B Substitute the underlined words with a word or words from the text. Make any grammatical changes which are necessary.

1 'Teacher assessments' <u>with</u> the national test results will show your child's achievements.
2 National standards are <u>listed</u> in the National Curriculum.
3 The same children's progress will be shown <u>in a period of years</u>.
4 The tests <u>are not designed for selection to</u> secondary schools.

C 1 What advantages and disadvantages can you see in compulsory testing on a National Curriculum?
   2 This is a letter to parents from the government. What effect do you think is intended by the use of adjectives like 'straightforward', 'basic', 'useful', 'clear', 'important'?

42   GUARANTEED DELIVERY

1   CHOICE OF THREE GUARANTEED SERVICES

Parcelforce offer you a choice of three guaranteed UK delivery services for urgent parcels. You don't need a contract –
simply hand them in at your nearest Parcelforce depot or
over the counter at many post offices.

You choose when it's delivered
PARCELFORCE DATAPOST guarantees delivery next morning by 10 am or Noon
PARCELFORCE 24 guarantees delivery by close of business
the next working day
PARCELFORCE 48 guarantees delivery within two
working days.

Remember, even if you've missed your last regular despatch deadline, there may still be time to take your parcels
to your local Parcelforce depot or accepting post office
counter.
   Call us free on **0800 22 44 66** for your nearest acceptance
address and latest acceptance time.

MONEY BACK GUARANTEE AND INCLUSIVE
COMPENSATION FOR LOSS OR DAMAGE
Whichever guaranteed service you use, we promise to deliver on time. In the unlikely event of delay, you may
claim a refund of the difference between the service level
selected and the service provided.

(from Parcelforce leaflet, 1995)

GLOSSARY

guarantee (heading) to make sure something will happen

Parcelforce (line 2) a parcels' delivery service run by the Post Office

depot (line 4) a place where a large number of goods are kept

working day (line 10) a workday, usually the weekdays Monday–Friday

despatch (lines 13–14) (also spelled 'dispatch'); to send to a person or destination (formal)

refund (line 23) to get back the money which you paid for something

LANGUAGE PRACTICE

A Put in the missing words. You can find all the words in the text. The first letters of the missing words are given.

1 This rapid service is designed for u____ parcels.
2 You should take your parcels and h____ t____ i____ to Parcelforce or at many post offices.
3 Parcelforce 24 will deliver on the next working day before c____ o____ b____.
4 For loss or damage, compensation and a m____ b____ guarantee is offered.
5 You don't pay to call 0800 224466 as this is a f____ number.
6 Our guarantee means we p____ to deliver on time.

B Substitute the underlined words with a word or words from the text. Make any grammatical changes which are necessary.

1 A written agreement is not required.
2 If you're too late for your normal despatch, you may be able to use this service.
3 With Parcelforce 48, delivery is no later than 48 hours during the week.
4 You can ask for money back if delivery is late.

C 1 If you wanted to send a parcel, why would you choose
      Parcelforce 24 or 48 rather than Datapost? Is there some-
      thing missing, in fact, from this information sheet?
   2 What would you say to Parcelforce if your parcel was
      lost, damaged, or delayed? Write a letter of about 50
      words.

---

43   LOCAL POLITICAL PARTY NEWS-SHEET

FOCUS   Liberal Democrats   No. 90
1 Contact: 109 Harrington Drive, Nottingham NG7 1 JL
   Tel: 505654
   **Editors: Andrew Ellwood, David George, Sheila
   Hobden,Councillor Gary Long**
5

PARKING NEAR QMC

Residents of streets near Queens Medical Centre have had
problems with the, often inconsiderate, parking of staff and
visitors to Queens Medical Centre. Cars parking on Derby
10 Road and between Hillside and Middleton Boulevard are
causing problems for traffic safety.
    To help with this problem the Council are proposing
to introduce double yellow lines on some parts of this road.
This should make driving safer BUT it is likely to make
15 the parking problems on Derby Road sliproad, Wollaton
Hall Drive and Wemyss Gardens worse. Gary has contacted the Council and asked them to review the whole
area.

Aslockton Drive: double yellow lines

The proposal for putting double yellow lines on one side of Aslockton Drive between Nuthall Road and Lutron Close has been advertised. As no objections were received the work will now go ahead. The yellow lines will make sure ambulances and other traffic can always get up the Drive.

Grassington Road warehouse: residents win another round

The residents of Grassington Road have won another round in their fight to stop the building of a large warehouse at the back of Grassington Road (on Astor Road). The firm's appeal to the Department of the Environment has been turned down. This supports the City Council's decision not to allow the warehouse.

The firm had a right to take the fight to the High Court within six weeks of that decision. As nothing has been heard in over two months, it is hoped that this is now the end of the matter. Once again our congratulations to the group of residents who have, it seems, won this fight.

Pavements on **Grimston Road**

The Focus Team have been contacted by local residents about the uneven state of the pavements on Grimston Road. David has written to the Council asking them to look at the problem.

Noise from **Dale Farm**

Local residents have reported that there is no improvement in the noise from the Dairy. Gary has contacted the Council and asked them what is happening.

Community Centre survey **Ainsley Estate**

The Focus Team survey on the need for facilities in the Ainsley area is nearly complete. The results will be in the next Focus.

(from *Focus*, News-sheet No. 90)

GLOSSARY

Liberal Democrats (line 2) a British political party formed from the Liberal Party and members of the Social Democratic Party in 1992

double yellow lines (line 14) pairs of lines painted along the side of the road to show that cars must not be parked

sliproad (line 16) a road which cars use to drive onto or off a motorway or other major road

warehouse (line 26) a large building where goods are stored before being sold

estate (line 48) a modern area of houses, usually all built at the same time and to the same design

facilities (line 49) services, buildings etc which people can use

GRAMMAR AND STYLE NOTE

Notice how the subjects of many paragraphs are either 'Residents' or 'The Focus Team'. This cleverly shows that the newsletter is a dialogue between the local political party and the voter.

LANGUAGE PRACTICE

A Put in the missing words. You can find all the words in the text. The first letters of the missing words are given.

1 Parked cars are causing a hazard to t____ s____.
2 Gary co____ the Council to ask for a review.
3 Because there were no objections, the work will g____ a____.
4 We are pleased by the residents' victory and offer our c____ to them.
5 Noise from Dale Farm Dairy is continuing. Residents say there is no im____.
6 The Focus Team survey into C____ C____ facilities needed for Ainsley is almost finished.

B Substitute the underlined words with a word or words from the text. Make any grammatical changes which are necessary.

1 There have been problems with <u>frequently selfish</u> car parking near Queens Medical Centre.

2 Grassington Road residents have <u>again been successful</u> in their fight against the proposed warehouse.

3 The firm's appeal has been <u>rejected</u>.

4 David has written asking the Council to <u>investigate</u>.

C 1 Write a letter to a local politician asking him or her to take action over a problem which is worrying you and your neighbours. Write about 50 words.

2 For each of the six problems reported here, say how effective you think the Focus Team's action has been, or whether there is no evidence of action by them.

Comparisons and Contrasts

44 MOROCCO

A

Morocco lies in the north-west corner of Africa. Its coast
borders the Mediterranean Sea and the Atlantic Ocean. The
Atlas Mountains cross Morocco from east to west. The
land near the sea is fertile, and most Moroccans live there
5 and farm the land. There are rich mineral deposits.

The land on the other side of the Atlas mountains is
part of the Sahara Desert. Three main groups of people
live in Morocco. The Berbers are mostly mountain herds-
men. The Arabs and the Moors (descendants of Arabs and
10 Berbers) live on the coastal plains.

Arabic is the official language of Morocco. Many people
speak French or Spanish. Morocco is a monarchy, governed
by parliament. The country's area was increased in the late
1970s when Morocco occupied Western (formerly Spanish)
15 Sahara. But some Saharans have fought against the occupation
of their country.

(from *Macmillan's Children's Encyclopaedia*, 1986)

B

If you'd like nothing better than stretching out in the sun
on a golden beach and doing absolutely nothing, there's
nowhere better to do it than Morocco.

Where you can find some of the most spectacular
5 beaches imaginable.

From the twin Atlantic and Mediterranean shores
around the legendary city of Tangier to the year round
sunshine of Agadir. Making it a paradise for sun-
worshippers.

10 Mind you, there could be one small problem that might

keep you away from the sea and sand, though obviously not from the sun.

Simply because a holiday in Morocco offers so much more to see and do.

Not just in the superb hotels, restaurants, and nightlife. 15
But in the discovery of the real Morocco.

Found in the exciting souks, exquisite palaces and the castellated casbahs that are never far away.

Bringing to colourful, bustling life over 2000 years of culture. 20

And creating a unique and thrilling environment that demands exploration. From both sightseer and seasider alike.

(from *The Sunday Express*, 26 February 1989)

GLOSSARY

A

fertile (line 4) land which is fertile is land on which things grow easily

herdsman (lines 8–9) someone who looks after a herd of animals

descendant (line 9) a descendant is someone who is related to people who lived a long time ago

monarchy (line 12) a country with a king or queen

B

legendary (line 7) something very famous, with a lot of stories told about it or about them

sun-worshipper (lines 8–9) someone who likes to spend a lot of time in the sun to get brown skin

nightlife (line 15) nightclubs, theatres, bars, etc, open at night

souk (line 17) a market-place in Muslim countries

exquisite (line 17) very beautiful

castellated (line 18) built like a castle

casbah (line 18) the citadel of a North African city

bustling (line 19) full of people and very busy

sightseer (line 22) someone who is travelling around in order to visit places of interest

Incomplete sentences Many sentences in the second Morocco text are incomplete. The most common structure is a subordinate clause which stands alone without its main clause, see, for example, lines 4–5 and 6–7. As a result the text sounds informal and conversational. For example, some of the clauses could be heard as answers to questions:

Q. Why do you go to Morocco?

A. Simply because a holiday in Morocco offers so much more to see and do. (lines 13–14)

Such a use of grammar involves the reader and increases interest in going to Morocco.

LANGUAGE PRACTICE

A Put in the missing words. You can find all the words in the text. The first letters of the missing words are given.

1 In the country there are rich mineral d____.
2 The moors are de____ of the Arabs.
3 The City of Tangier is l____.
4 Such a thrilling place demands ex____.
5 The castles are beautiful and the palaces exq____.
6 The beaches are sp____.

B Substitute the underlined words with a word or words from the text. Make any grammatical changes which are necessary.

1 Most Moroccans live there and are farmers on the land.
2 The Saharans fought against their country being occupied.
3 It is a unique environment which demands to be explored.
4 It is a paradise for those who like to worship the sun.

C Write a brief description of one aspect of your country (about 25 words). Your description should be for junior schoolchildren who may read the description in an encyclopaedia or geography book. Then rewrite the same description (another 25 words) so that it can be used in a brochure for tourists.

45   THE BIBLE

A

And now I will show you the best way of all.   1

I may speak in tongues of men or of angels, but if I am
without love, I am a sounding gong or a clanging cymbal.
I may have the gift of prophecy, and know every hidden
truth; I may have faith strong enough to move mountains;   5
but if I have no love, I am nothing. I may dole out all I
possess, or even give my body to be burnt, but if I have no
love, I am none the better.

Love is patient; love is kind and envies no one. Love is
never boastful, nor conceited, nor rude; never selfish, not   10
quick to take offence. Love keeps no score of wrongs; does
not gloat over other men's sins, but delights in the truth.
There is nothing love cannot face; there is no limit to its
faith, its hope and its endurance.

Love will never come to an end. Are there prophets?   15
their work will be over. Are there tongues of ecstasy? they
will cease. Is there knowledge? it will vanish away; for our
knowledge and our prophecy alike are partial, and the partial vanishes when wholeness comes. When I was a child,
my speech, my outlook and my thought were all childish.   20
When I grew up, I had finished with childish things. Now
we see only puzzling reflections in a mirror, but then we
shall see face to face. My knowledge now is partial; then it
will be whole, like God's knowledge of me. In a word,
there are three things that last for ever: faith, hope and   25
love; but the greatest of them all is love.

(First letter of Paul to the Corinthians xiii, 1–13:
The New English Bible, 1961)

B

1   . . . and yet shew I unto you a more excellent way.

Though I speak with the tongues of men and of angels, and have not charity, I am become as sounding brass, or a tinkling cymbal.

5   And though I have the gift of prophecy, and understand all mysteries, and all knowledge; and though I have all faith, so that I could remove mountains, and have not charity, I am nothing.

And though I bestow all my goods to feed the poor,
10   and though I give my body to be burned, and have not charity, it profiteth me nothing.

Charity suffereth long, and is kind; charity envieth not; charity vaunteth not itself, is not puffed up,

Doth not behave itself unseemly, seeketh not her own,
15   is not easily provoked, thinketh no evil;

Rejoiceth not in iniquity, but rejoiceth in the truth;

Beareth all things, believeth all things, hopeth all things, endureth all things.

Charity never faileth: but whether there be prophecies,
20   they shall fail; whether there be tongues, they shall cease; whether there be knowledge, it shall vanish away.

For we know in part, and we prophesy in part.

But when that which is perfect is come, then that which is in part shall be done away.

25   When I was a child, I spake as a child, I understood as a child, I thought as a child: but when I became a man, I put away childish things.

For now we see through a glass, darkly; but then face to face: now I know in part; but then I shall know even as
30   also I am known.

And now abideth faith, hope, charity, these three; but the greatest of these is charity.

(First epistle of Paul to the Corinthians xiii, 1–13:
Authorized Version of *The Bible*, 1611)

GLOSSARY

A

speak in tongues (line 2) the power of speaking in unknown languages

gong (line 3) a flat piece of metal. You hit it with a hammer and it makes a sound like a bell

cymbal (line 3) thin, circular piece of metal. You strike two together when playing them as a musical instrument

dole out (line 6) give willingly and generously

gloat (line 12) to take pleasure in your own success and in the failure of others

ecstasy (line 16) very deep pleasure

partial (line 18) only a part, not the whole

B

shew (line 1) show

charity (line 3) kindness to other people. In the Bible the word is best translated as love for others

profiteth (line 11) profits; the 's' ending of the third person singular is '-eth' or '-the' in earlier stages of the language (here the early seventeenth century)

vaunteth (line 13) to display, to boast

puffed up (line 13) thinking itself important

doth (line 14) does

unseemly (line 14) in an unsuitable way

iniquity (line 16) a state in which things are not equal

endureth (line 18) to last for a long time

vanish (line 21) disappear

glass (line 28) another word for mirror; it is now rather dated

abideth (line 31) to exist for a long time

LANGUAGE PRACTICE

A Put in the missing words. You can find all the words in the text. The first letters of the missing words are given.

1 Love is kind, envies no one and is p____.
2 My knowledge is not complete; it is only par____.

3 At that time my thoughts and outlook on life were ch____.

4 The reflections in the mirror were p____.

5 Now I can see things f____ to f____.

6 We should not gl____ over other people's sins or misfortunes.

B Rewrite the following words and phrases from early seventeenth-century English into modern English.

1 It profiteth me nothing.

2 I shew unto you a more excellent way.

3 I am become as sounding brass.

4 Charity envieth not.

C Give two reasons why holy books like *The Bible* are needed by a society or culture.

---

46 PIT BULL ATTACK

A

1 MAN CRITICAL AFTER PIT BULL ATTACK

A man was critically ill in hospital with facial injuries last night after being savaged by two pit bull terriers. Police shot dead one of the dogs.

Frank Tempest, aged 54, of Lincoln was attacked as he walked home from work. Police warned people to stay indoors as 20 police officers, six armed, hunted for the dogs. One animal was shot and the other caught and destroyed.

Describing Mr Tempest's injuries, a police spokesman said: 'You wouldn't recognize it as a human face – it is positively horrendous.'

Police said the owner of the dogs could not be prosecuted as both were dead.

Dame Janet Fookes, Conservative MP for Plymouth Drake, said the Government should introduce compulsory dog registration. ₁₅

(from The Guardian, 9 May 1991)

B

DOGS RIP A MAN'S NOSE OFF ₁

HORROR ATTACK!
By **Martin Stote**

COPS shot two savage pit bull terriers yesterday after they gored a man's face to shreds. ₅

The escaped devil-dogs tore into shift worker Frank Tempest, 54, as he walked home at dawn.

Shocked witnesses said the hell hounds RIPPED OFF his nose, MAULED his ear and TORE skin off his face.

The dogs ambushed father-of-four Frank, then dragged ₁₀ him screaming along the road as he struggled to fight them off.

Police sealed off the street and warned terrified neighbours to stay indoors as the marauding dogs savaged a cat to death. ₁₅

Then six police marksmen with automatic rifles blasted the dogs, believed to be a bitch and her pup, with a hail of bullets.

One pit bull was shot dead, the other wounded and trailed for an hour before being killed. ₂₀

Both had escaped from a house close to despatch loader Frank's home in Monk's Road Lincoln.

**Police refused to name the owner last night and
said he would NOT face prosecution.**

(from *The Daily Star*, 9 May 1991)

GLOSSARY

A

attack (heading) bite or hit suddenly and without any warning
critical (line 1) very ill
facial injuries (line 2) injuries to the face
savaged (line 3) attacked violently
pit bull terriers (line 3) a breed of fighting dogs
positively horrendous (line 11) very bad
prosecute (line 12) to bring criminal charges against someone
compulsory (line 15) something that must be done
dog registration (line 16) a plan to have every dog put on a government list

B

cops (line 4) police (informal)
gored (line 5) wound someone badly with horns, tusks, or teeth
shreds (line 5) small pieces
tore into (line 6) cut
shift worker (line 6) someone who works sometimes during the
   day and sometimes during the night
hound (line 8) dog
mauled (line 9) to be attacked by an animal
sealed off (line 12) prevented people from getting into a place by
   blocking all the entrances
marauding (line 14) looking for something to steal or kill
marksman (line 16) someone who can fire a gun very accurately
rifle (line 16) a kind of gun
blasted (line 16) shot
bitch (line 17) a female dog
pup (line 17) puppy (abbreviation), young dog
despatch loader (line 20) someone who loads vans and lorries

GRAMMAR AND STYLE NOTES

1 The two newspapers are written in different styles. *The Daily Star* is a popular newspaper
with millions of readers daily, *The Guardian* is not read as widely. It appeals to readers who
prefer more analyses of a wider range of news. *The Sun* (see texts 47A and 48A) is a very

similar newspaper to *The Daily Star*. The language used by *The Daily Star* (and *The Sun*) is more sensational and is designed to capture readers' interest.

2 Notice the use of vocabulary in *The Daily Star* which stresses the violence of the events and the strongly emotional reactions. For example 'gored ... to shreds'; 'devil–dogs'; 'hell hounds'; 'tore into'; 'ripped off'; 'mauled'; 'marauding'; 'screaming'; 'blasted'.

LANGUAGE PRACTICE

A Put in the missing words. You can find all the words in the text. The first letters of the missing words are given.

    1 He is cr____ ill in hospital.
    2 He has serious f____ injuries.
    3 The owner of the dogs would not be p____.
    4 The government should introduce com____ dog registration.
    5 The dog a____ the man as he was walking home from work.
    6 Police s____ off the street and warned people to stay indoors.

B Substitute the underlined words with a word or words from the text. Make any grammatical changes which are necessary.

    1 They attacked Frank who was a <u>father of four</u>.
    2 They warned <u>the neighbours, who were terrified</u>, to stay indoors.
    3 <u>The house from which they had both escaped was close to Frank's house</u>.
    4 Then they dragged him <u>along the road. He was screaming</u>.

C Do you think all dangerous dogs should be killed and not be allowed to breed?

47   CHARLES AND DIANA

A

1 **Prince Charles and Princess Di will never be King and Queen after the sensational announcement of their separation, MPs said last night**.

Westminster was united in predicting Charles will step
5 aside – and leave eldest son Prince William to take the throne alone.

MPs of all parties claimed the couple's split was the first step to divorce and had put paid to the Prince fulfilling his destiny as King Charles III.

10 Gasps of disbelief greeted Mr Major's Commons claim – after he made the official announcement – that the Royal separation would not stop Di being crowned.

He told MPs: 'The succession to the throne is unaffected. There is no reason why the Princess of Wales should
15 not be crowned Queen in due course.'

The Premier was backed by Buckingham Palace, which said the couple would not divorce.

(from *The Sun*, 12 November 1992)

B

1 The separation of the Prince and Princess of Wales produced widespread public sympathy last night, mingled with astonishment at official insistence that the decision will have 'no constitutional implications' for the monarchy.

The marriage break-up brings to an end all the mar-
5 riages of the Queen's children. Prince Charles and Princess Diana, who married on a tide of popular enthusiasm in 1981, will continue to carry out limited public engagements together, including dinner for Edinburgh summit leaders

on the royal yacht tomorrow night. They will share respon- 10
sibility for raising their two sons.

But they will live apart, the princess at Kensington
Palace, Prince Charles at Highgrove in Gloucestershire and
Clarence House, the Queen Mother's London residence.

'The Queen and the Duke of Edinburgh, though sad- 15
dened, understand and sympathise with the difficulties that
have led to this decision,' Buckingham Palace said.

(from *The Guardian*, 12 November 1992)

GLOSSARY

A

Di (line 1) Diana (abbreviation)

separation (line 3) when a couple who are married decide to
live apart

MPs (line 3) Members of Parliament (abbreviation)

Westminster (line 4) a district of London where the Houses of
Parliament are situated

throne (line 6) a throne is a large, decorated chair used by a King
or Queen for special ceremonies and events. The word also
refers to the position of being the King or Queen of a country

split (line 7) separation (informal)

put paid to (line 8) ensured it could not happen

Commons claim (line 10) a claim made in the House of Commons

succession (line 13) the next person to be King or Queen

unaffected (lines 13–14) not changed in any way

Premier (line 16) the Prime Minister

backed (line 16) supported by

Buckingham Palace (line 16) the main residence and office of the
British King or Queen

B

mingled with (line 2) mixed with

insistence (line 3) to say very firmly that something must be
done or is true

break-up (line 5) separation (informal)
tide of popular enthusiasm (line 7) the support of the majority of
    people at that time
summit (line 9) a meeting at which the leaders of two or more
    countries discuss important matters

GRAMMAR AND STYLE NOTE

It is common in formal English for statements to be made by a well-known place or public
institution, even though, of course, people in those places make the statements. (See text A,
line 16 and text B, line 17).

LANGUAGE PRACTICE

A Put in the missing words. You can find all the words in the
   text. The first letters of the missing words are given.

   1 The announcement of their separation was sen____.
   2 The Royal separation will not stop Di being c____.
   3 The succession to the throne is un____.
   4 They will share responsibility for r____ their two sons.
   5 They will continue to carry out limited public en____.
   6 They sympathize with the d____ that have led to this
      decision.

B Substitute the underlined words with a word or words
   from the text. Make any grammatical changes which are
   necessary.

   1 It will not affect the <u>next person to be King or Queen</u>.
   2 They will <u>both be responsible for bringing up their
      two sons</u>.
   3 They will <u>no longer live in the same house together</u>
      but will not divorce.
   4 She will continue to <u>undertake limited public duties</u>.

C Should a future King and Queen divorce or should they
   stay together for the future of the country? Discuss with a
   partner who has read the text and then write 30–40 words
   in answer to this question.

48 AUSTRALIAN PRIME MINISTER

A

LIZARD OF OZ

1

Fury as premier bashes war Brits

AUSSIE Prime Minister Paul Keating was branded a 'buffoon' last night over his outrageous slur on Britain's war heroes.

5

Motormouth Keating told his Parliament Britain had 'deserted' Australia during the struggle against the Japanese in 1942.

The insult followed hot on the heels of his rudeness to the Queen during her official visit.

10

Labour MP Ted Leadbetter stormed in the Commons, 'The Australian Prime Minister has behaved like an utter buffoon.

'He has no sense of manners, no sense of courtesy and a total disregard for history and our strong connections with Australia.'

15

Premier John Major stepped in and promised to do all he could to defuse the 'unhappy situation'.

He is anxious that the affair should not blow up into a full scale clash between the governments of the two countries.

20

(from *The Sun*, 28 February 1992)

B

ANGER AT KEATING CLAIM THAT BRITAIN BETRAYED AUSTRALIA

1

PAUL KEATING, the Australian Prime Minister, yesterday unleashed a political furore with a strong attack on

Britain's record in Asia during the Second World War, accusing it of abandoning Australia to the Japanese.

Mr Keating's public outburst, unprecedented for an Australian leader, came in a heated debate in the federal parliament in Canberra, when he defended himself against the accusation that he had shown no respect for the Queen during her Australian visit.

In comments which infuriated British and Australian MPs, Mr Keating declared: 'I learned about self-respect and self-regard for Australia, not about cultural cringe to a country which decided not to defend the Malayan peninsula, not to worry about Singapore and not to give us our troops back to keep ourselves from Japanese domination.'

As some MPs shouted support and others tried to howl him down, Mr Keating accused the opposition Liberal Party of holding on to 'kowtowing' attitudes towards Britain from the 1950s.

(from *The Guardian*, 28 February 1992)

GLOSSARY

A

lizard (line 1) a small reptile

Oz (line 1) Australia (informal)

bashes (line 2) criticizes (informal)

Brits (line 2) Britons (informal)

Aussie (line 3) Australian (also spelled 'Ossie' or 'Ozzie') (informal)

buffoon (line 4) someone who does stupid things

slur (line 4) an insulting remark which could damage someone's reputation

motormouth (line 6) someone who talks too much

desert (line 7) to leave in a cowardly way

hot on the heels (line 9) very soon afterwards

defuse (line 18) make a situation less dangerous or tense

clash (line 20) a confrontation

B

furore (line 4) a very angry or excited reaction by people to something

unprecedented (line 7) not happened before

federal (line 8) when a group of states is controlled by a central government

infuriate (line 12) to make angry

cringe (line 14) an excessively polite and respectful manner

howl down (line 18) to shout in such a way that people cannot hear

kowtowing (line 20) behaving very humbly and respectfully towards someone, especially when hoping to get something from them

GRAMMAR AND STYLE NOTES

1 See p 150 for discussion of vocabulary and the choices of informal, strongly emotional, and violent and one-syllable words, especially verbs, in *The Sun* (for example, 'blow up', 'clash' and 'bashes').

2 The report in *The Sun* also uses transitive verbs which have Mr Keating as the subject. This makes clear that Keating is clearly and directly responsible. For example, Premier '*bashes* war Brits'. *The Guardian* is more careful in its report and nouns are preferred to verbs. There are still a number of transitive verbs used, however (for example, 'unleashed a political furore').

LANGUAGE PRACTICE

A Put in the missing words. You can find all the words in the text. The first letters of the missing words are given.

    1 His slur on British war heroes was out____.

    2 He was criticized for a total dis____ for history.

    3 He promised to try to de____ the situation.

    4 He is anxious that the affair should not blow up into a full scale c____.

    5 His comments in____ the government.

    6 He has shown no res____ for the Queen.

B Answer the following questions. The answers to the questions all contain a specialist word or phrase. All the words appear in the text.

    1 What are the informal words for Australian and Australia?

2   What is an informal word for the English?

3   *The Wizard of Oz* is a famous Hollywood film. In the
    film Oz is a magic land. In this headline what word
    replaces Wizard?

4   What kind of parliament is the Australian parliament?

C   Is it right that the British Queen should also be queen of a
    country on the other side of the world? Give one reason
    why and one reason why not.

---

49   MANSLAUGHTER

A

1   MAJOR'S WIFE ADMITS RUNNING DOWN LOVER

The wife of a major who killed her husband's German lover
by mowing her down and running her over in her car had
her plea of manslaughter through diminished responsibility
accepted by a British court martial in Germany yesterday.

Christine Dryland was formally found not guilty of mur-
dering 34-year-old Marika Sparfeld. A charge of attempting
to murder her husband, Anthony Dryland, was withdrawn.

The court martial in First Armoured Division headquar-
ters at Verden, near Bremen, was adjourned until tomorrow to hear medical evidence.

Mrs Dryland ran down Miss Sparfeld on her husband's
46th birthday; a few days after he announced he was leaving
her to live with the secretary who was a freelance equestrian
journalist.

She drove over the body a number of times, according to
witnesses. She also drove at her husband, hurling him on to the
bonnet, but he escaped with cuts and bruises in the incident at
Soltau riding club, near Hanover.

She is being tried under English law. If a prison sentence is passed, she will serve it in England. The verdict will be decided by a panel of four women and three men, with a vice-judge advocate general taking an advisory role.

(from *The Guardian*, 26 February 1992)

B

GRIEF OF THE LOVE CHEAT MAJOR

Daily vigil at grave of blonde killed by wife

Romeo Major Tony Dryland – whose wife faced a court martial yesterday for killing his German lover – is a broken man destroyed by grief, friends said last night.

He cannot stop mourning blonde Marika Sparfeld, 34, who died in his arms after she was crushed beneath a car driven by spurned mum-of-two Christine Dryland.

Every day, the major cycles to Marika's grave in the hillside cemetery above the Rhine Army barracks in Soltau, where he is stationed. His lonely, hunched figure has become a familiar sight to German locals as he renews the fresh flowers beside the headstone.

Riding fanatic Dryland, 46, has also left a brown and white toy pony by the grave as a reminder of his Marika's love of horses.

Since the tragedy last July, Dryland has not spoken to Christine, 42.

And at yesterday's military court martial in Verden, their eyes never met.

Dryland stood stiffly six feet from Christine as she admitted manslaughter due to diminished responsibility.

Her plea of not guilty to murder was accepted. She will be sentenced tomorrow.

(from *The Daily Mail*, 26 February 1992)

GLOSSARY

A

manslaughter (heading) to kill someone accidentally, when you intend to hurt or injure them

diminished responsibility (line 4) to be mentally ill and not know what you are doing

court martial (line 9) to try someone for a crime in a military court

adjourned (line 10) to stop for a short time

freelance (line 14) someone who is not employed by a single organization

equestrian (line 14) to do with horses

advocate (line 24) a lawyer who defends someone in a court of law

B

Romeo (line 3) a passionate male lover or seducer

spurned (line 9) rejected

barracks (line 11) buildings where members of the armed forces live and work

hunched (line 12) raising your shoulders and hanging your head in a sad way

fanatic (line 15) someone who does something with great enthusiasm

plea (line 24) to say if you have or have not committed a crime

sentenced (line 25) given a particular punishment for a crime

LANGUAGE PRACTICE

A Put in the missing words. You can find all the words in the text. The first letters of the missing words are given.

  1 She was found not g____.
  2 The court martial was ad____ until tomorrow.
  3 The secretary was a fr____ journalist.
  4 She is being t____ under English law.
  5 She will be s____ tomorrow.
  6 He is stationed at army b____ in Soltau.

B   Answer the following questions. The answers to the questions all contain a specialist word or phrase. All the words appear in the text.

1   What is the legal expression for killing someone when the intention was to hurt or injure them?
2   What is a military trial in a military court called?
3   What is the phrase used to describe someone who is mentally or psychologically ill when a crime is committed?
4   What is the legal word used to describe the answer given to a charge of 'guilty' or 'not guilty'?

C   Write a brief paragraph (about 50 words) in which you summarize the events described in these two newspaper reports.

---

50   LETTERS

A

POSTCARD HOME   1

Menorca   2 August, 1995

Hi everybody! Hope you are all well. I'm fine. Weather is up and down. We've had thunder and heavy rain and now it's really hot and sunny again. Hotel is OK. Nice view   5 and nice little beach with clear water. Food is good. Lots of buffets but don't like Spanish dishes much. Cokes are over a £1 a can!! Must go now. Miss you.
    See you soon,
        Jenn   10
        XX

                                            (Author's data)

B

LETTER OF APPLICATION
15 Dover Court
Edgbaston B15 2TT
0121–9762020

5 Dear Sir,

I enclose an application form and current CV for a position
in your hotel.

I have four GCSEs and have recently completed 15 months
working with McDonald's Restaurants. During this time I
10 successfully achieved my five stars which means I passed all
my relevant tests and training courses. Gaining these stars
(certificates) means I have achieved the required standards
of food preparation and customer service.

I am interested in a career in Hotel and Catering and would
15 welcome the opportunity of an apprenticeship (with NVQ
training) or of direct employment with you.

The Hotel and Catering Company (HCTC) in Birmingham
would be able to arrange an apprenticeship. My contact is
Mark Rowlands. His working address is:

20   Four Seasons House, 26–30 Heathcote Street,
            Birmingham, B9 2AA.
            (Tel: 0121 9484440)

Alternatively, please contact me at the above telephone
number.

25 I am willing to work very hard and to learn quickly. I am
very keen to succeed in this area of work.

   Yours faithfully,
      Matthew Fry

                                        (Author's data)

GLOSSARY

A

Menorca (line 2) an island in the Mediterranean sea which belongs to Spain

up and down (line 4) an informal phrase meaning that something is always changing

Coke (line 7) Coca-Cola; a fizzy soft drink

B

CV (line 6) curriculum vitae (abbreviation). This is a Latin phrase meaning a written record about yourself, your qualifications etc

catering (line 14) providing food and drink for large numbers of people

apprenticeship (line 15) working with people with more experience in order to learn particular skills from them

NVQ (line 15) National Vocational Qualification (abbreviation)

alternatively (line 23) on the other hand (formal)

GRAMMAR AND STYLE NOTES

1 Note the use of ellipsis on the 'Postcard Home'. This is another communication between people who know each other well. See comments on ellipsis on pp.12 and 88. 'Must go now' and 'Miss you' have the personal pronoun 'I' missing; 'Nice view'; 'Nice little beach' have subject and main verb missing ('There is') and 'Hotel is OK' has the definite article ellipted.

2 It would be inappropriate if there were similar ellipsis in a letter of application for a job.

LANGUAGE PRACTICE

A Put in the missing words. You can find all the words in the text. The first letters of the missing words are given.

1 The weather is u____ and down.
2 The hotel offers lots of b____ and the food is good.
3 I don't like Spanish d____ much.
4 I enclose a copy of my c____ CV.
5 I would welcome the opportunity of an app____ with you.
6 Alt____, please contact me at the above telephone number.

B Substitute the underlined words with a word or words from the text. Make any grammatical changes which are necessary.

1 Attractive small beach with clear water.
2 The food is good. There are lots of buffets.
3 I passed all my appropriate examinations.
4 I enclose a record of my personal details for a job in your hotel.

C Write a postcard home from a place you have recently visited. Use an informal style (30 words). Then rewrite the same content in a formal style as if you were writing to someone you do not know well (30 words).

ANSWERS

PERSUASIVE AND ADVERTISING LANGUAGE

1 Trainers for Women
A 1 cushion; versatile; rugged 2 trainer 3 aerobics 4 challenge;
compromise 5 hiking 6 recycled
B 1 a serious hiking shoe 2 his life support 3 compromise 4 train

2 American Jeep
A 1 traction 2 secure 3 brake 4 rough 5 cruise 6 four-wheel
B 1 the locals 2 creature comforts 3 are more expensive 4 venture
further afield

3 US Armed Forces Ad
A 1 ambitious 2 fields 3 eligible 4 glimpse 5 skills 6 talent
B 1 won't recognize yourself 2 smart move 3 put aside 4 specialties

4 Mobile Phones Ad
A range; call waiting; contact; PIN; permission; duration; costs;
records; answering machine
B 1 there is a bleep tone 2 call barring 3 call timer; battery strength;
signal strength 4 call divert

5 Small Ads: Lake District
A 1 Attractive Cotts for Xmas and NY. Ideal families
2 Lge lux rooms. Teamkrs
3 Cotts. Superb locs. Slp 4/6; Ambleside 2 mls
4 £15 pp/pn. Min 2 nts
5 Rooms with CTV
6 DB + B fr £50 pp
B 1 lavish 2 tranquil 3 brochure 4 elegance; style

6 Academic Book Catalogue
A 1 sociolinguistics 2 integral 3 varies 4 catalogue 5 hardback;
paperback 6 reader
B 1 a relatively new field 2 c £25 3 topics 4 viewed as an act of
communication

NEWS REPORTING AND JOURNALISM

13 Sports Report: Basketball

A 1 shaky; questionable 2 eliminated 3 underscored 4 improbable
5 indisputably 6 exceptionally
B 1 center 2 basket 3 NBA 4 dunk

14 Sports Report: Football

A 1 lethal; anxious 2 tentative 3 daft 4 defending 5 agonizingly
6 dodgy
B 1 penalty 2 pen 3 att 4 injury time

15 Soaraway Psion

A 1 demand 2 turn out 3 sources 4 substantial 5 vital 6 peak
B 1 bullish AGM statement 2 vital memory chips 3 surge 4 turn out
more hand-held computers

16 Editorial

A 1 impoverished; abuses 2 light 2 glib 4 tortured 5 rights
6 tolerated
B 1 well-founded suspicion of military wrongdoing 2 for his life
3 made the murder public 4 died in mysterious circumstances

17 Children and Cartoons

A 1 dominate 2 violent; larger-than-life 3 subtle 4 unmistakable
5 gloomy 6 evilness
B 1 depict a violent storyline 2 unmistakable 3 incredibly complex to
comprehend 4 it is far too easy to simply dismiss these cartoons

18 Pop Music Review

A 1 worthy 2 oddities 3 album 4 unpredictable 5 material 6
spontaneous
B 1 thanks to 2 setting rock's pace 3 once and for all 4 trio

19 Dow Dampens Asia Markets

A 1 recovered 2 fall 3 key 4 steady 5 gains 6 dampened
B 1 bullish 2 broker 3 blue-chip company 4 Nikkei; Hang Seng; Wall
Street

MAGAZINE LANGUAGE

20 Horoscope

A 1 accusation 2 seize 3 discriminating 4 fall 5 wrestle 6 solution; persevere

B 1 feel a strong urge to 2 wrestling with 3 in the longer term 4 win through in the end

21 Just Testing (Woks)

A 1 results 2 accessories 3 enamelled 4 flimsy 5 resistant 6 value

B 1 chopsticks 2 aluminium 3 wok 4 bamboo

22 Dating

A 1 disaster 2 specific 3 sell; short 4 lament 5 walk 6 quality

B 1 guy 2 dumb 3 movie 4 mom

23 Beauty Tips

A 1 tips 2 word; mouth 3 boost 4 salon 5 mascara 6 features

B 1 eyeshadow 2 lip balm 3 blowdry 4 mascara

24 Problem Pages

A 1 let down 2 condescending 3 agony 4 green 5 trapped 6 ex-boyfriend

B 1 wondering what to say to comfort her 2 they're confronted with suffering and death 3 to pretend that nothing has happened 4 are not interested in seeing other guys

25 American Topics: A Doctor at 17

A 1 graduated 2 native 3 grapevine 4 ping pong 5 open minded 6 co-authored

B 1 math 2 opthalmology 3 intern 4 Nobel Prize

TECHNICAL LANGUAGE

26 Car Handbook

A 1 multigrade 2 temperate climate 3 frictional 4 temperatures 5 unavoidable 6 restriction

B 1 reasonably priced 2 have in addition the following advantages 3 not generally acceptable 4 in the case of high annual mileage

27 Flymo Guarantee: Information Sheet

A 1 purchase 2 automatically 3 terms 4 incurred 5 Network 6 proof of purchase

B 1 cover 2 12 months period 3 require the following information 4 purchased from

28 Internal Fax/Memo

A 1 deal; laptop 2 executive 3 quote 4 fax 5 pipeline 6 hard disk

B 1 cc 2 memo 3 quote 4 Mb 5 MD 6 e:mail

29 Marrow (Sowing Guide)

A 1 excellent 2 firm 3 stage 4 harvest 5 swell 6 standard

B 1 cover with (a) fine layer of compost 2 promote further fruit development 3 tip 4 subject to

30 Birth Certificate

A 1 chargeable 2 date of birth 3 registrar 4 sub–district 5 caution 6 identity

B 1 do hereby certify 2 an offence to falsify a 3 to the prejudice of any person 4 is not evidence

FOOD AND DRINK ENGLISH

31 Menu: Fast Food Restaurant

A 1 flavour 2 varieties 3 main course 4 French fries 5 breakfast 6 milk shakes

B 1 extra value meals 2 side order 3 beverages 4 regular

32 Sandwich Loaf Wrapper

A 1 characteristically 2 starch; protein 3 well balanced diet 4 wholemeal 5 slice 6 deep freeze

B 1 different proportions 2 keep this wrapper away from 3 ingredient 4 best before

33 Soft Drink Can

A 1 registered trade mark 2 calorie controlled diet 3 fat 4 ice cold 5 freephone 6 recycle

B 1 artificial sweetener 2 best before end date 3 under authority 4 is available in UK mainland only

34 Wine Label
A 1 quality bottled 2 reputation 3 pioneered 4 harvested 5 straw; tints 6 distinctive
B 1 is the country's largest exporter 2 of consistency 3 owes much 4 nose; palate is dry

35 Recipe for Chocolate Banana Pudding
A 1 mashed 2 skimmed 3 consistency 4 transfer 5 topping up 6 turn out
B 1 lightly grease 2 fold in sufficient 3 cooked through 4 maker's instructions

THE LANGUAGE OF INFORMATION

36 Film Features
A 1 high-stakes 2 caveman 3 century 4 avenge 5 acclaimed 6 unwittingly
B 1 goes along for the ride 2 is in a fight against time; on time 3 to toe the line 4 the late

37 TV Page
A 1 pays dividends 2 archives 3 live 4 ceasefire 5 patriarch 6 weather
B 1 general knowledge quiz 2 triple bill 3 steps into his boss's shoes 4 reviews

38 Hotel Information
A 1 worship 2 early morning call 3 onward reservation 4 prior arrangements 5 required 6 vending machine
B 1 invite all comments 2 the accounts of . . . should be settled direct 3 your mail can be stamped by 4 normal retail prices

39 Milk Message
A 1 Dairy Industry 2 Marque 3 at present 4 community 5 very competitively 6 coupons
B 1 protect our service relationship with you 2 our unique British service 3 held back 4 effective date of the new prices is 30 October 1994

A 1 sunshine 2 widespread 3 largely 4 wintry 5 visibility 6 summary
B 1 The BBC's 2 from time to time 3 be light to moderate 4 with hail or sleet

41 National School Tests
A 1 got on 2 fall short 3 across 4 basics 5 year-olds 6 aiming for
B 1 set alongside 2 set out 3 in time 4 it is not the purpose of the tests to select children for

42 Guaranteed Delivery
A 1 urgent 2 hand them in 3 close of business 4 money back 5 free 6 promise
B 1 you don't need a contract 2 you've missed 3 within two working days 4 may claim a refund

43 Local Party Political News-sheet
A 1 traffic safety 2 contacted 3 go ahead 4 congratulations 5 improvement 6 community centre
B 1 often inconsiderate 2 won another round 3 turned down 4 look at the problem

COMPARISONS AND CONTRASTS

44 Morocco
A 1 deposits 2 descendants 3 legendary 4 exploration 5 exquisite 6 spectacular
B 1 farm the land 2 the occupation of their country 3 demands exploration 4 sun-worshippers

45 The Bible
A 1 patient 2 partial 3 childish 4 puzzling 5 face to face 6 gloat
B 1 It does not profit me; I do not profit 2 I will show you the best way of all 3 I am a sounding gong 4 love envies no one

46 Pit Bull Attack
A 1 critically 2 facial 3 prosecuted 4 compulsory 5 ambushed/ attacked 6 sealed
B 1 father-of-four Frank 2 the terrified neighbours 3 both had escaped from a house close to Frank's home 4 along the road screaming

47 Charles and Diana

A 1 sensational 2 crowned 3 unaffected 4 raising 5 engagements
6 difficulties

B 1 succession 2 share responsibility for raising their two sons
3 separate 4 carry out limited public engagements

48 Australian Prime Minister

A 1 outrageous 2 disregard 3 defuse 4 confrontation 5 infuriated
6 respect

B 1 Oz; Aussie 2 Brits 3 Lizard 4 federal

49 Manslaughter

A 1 guilty 2 adjourned 3 freelance 4 tried 5 sentenced 6 barracks

B 1 manslaughter 2 court martial 3 someone with diminished
responsibility 4 plea

50 Letters

A 1 up 2 buffets 3 dishes 4 current 5 apprenticeship 6 alternatively

B 1 nice little beach with clear water 2 food good; lots of buffets 3 all
my relevant tests 4 a CV for a position in your hotel

ACKNOWLEDGEMENTS

The publishers make grateful acknowledgement to the following for permission to reproduce copyright material:

p. 5: by permission of Chrysler Jeep/Delaney Fletcher Bozell; p. 10: by permission of Dixons Stores Group; p. 18: *Polity Press Book Catalogue*, Blackwell Publishers, Oxford; p. 20: by permission of The Insurance Service; p. 23: by permission of Friends of the Earth; p. 26: by permission of British Airways Holidays; p. 34: 'Putting the bite on Big Mac' by Pauline Springett, *The Guardian*, 16 May 1995; p. 39: 'Make Jordan and his Bulls disappear' by Michael Wilbon, *International Herald Tribune*, 20 May 1995, © 1995 The Washington Post, reprinted with permission; p. 42: 'Palmer shoots down warbling canaries' by John Wilford, *The Observer*, 7 May 1995; p. 48: 'Guatemala: a pattern of duplicity', *The New York Times*, 19 May 1995, copyright © 1995 by The New York Times Company, reprinted by permission; p. 54: 'Sidi joins the pace-setters' by Charles Shaar Murray, *The Daily Telegraph*, 6 May 1995, reprinted by permission of Charles Shaar Murray; p. 62: 'Your stars' by Jonathan Cainer, *Woman*, reprinted by permission of Jonathan Cainer; p. 65: 'Fry and mighty', *The Daily Mail*, 24 September 1994, reprinted by permission of Solo Syndication Limited; p. 77: 'American topics: a doctor at 17', *International Herald Tribune*, 20 May 1995, reprinted with permission from International Herald Tribune; p. 89: by permission of W. W. Johnson & Son Limited; p. 96: by permission of McDonald's; p. 99: by permission of J. Sainsbury plc; p. 103: by permission of Coca-Cola Great Britain and Ireland; p. 106: by permission of The House of Seagram; p. 108 'Chocolate banana pudding', *Woman*, reprinted by permission of Woman Magazine; p. 131:

National Testing and Assessment in Schools in 1995, Crown copyright is reproduced with the permission of the Controller of HMSO; p. 134: by permission of Parcelforce; p. 136: *Focus*, by permission of Liberal Democrats, Nottingham; p. 145: *Revised English Bible*, © Oxford University and Cambridge University Presses, 1989; p. 148: 'Man critical after pit bull attack', *The Guardian*, 9 May 1991; p. 149: 'Dogs rip a man's nose off' by Martin Stote, *The Daily Star*, 9 May 1991; p. 152: article by Trevor Kavanagh and Simon Walters, *The Sun*, 12 November 1992; p. 152: article from *The Guardian*, 12 November 1992; p. 155: 'Lizard of Oz' by John Kay and David Kemp, *The Sun*, 28 February 1992; p. 155: 'Anger at Keating claim that Britain betrayed Australia' by Robert Milliken, *The Guardian*, 28 February 1992; p. 158: 'Major's wife admits running down lover', *The Guardian*, 26 February 1992; p. 159: 'Grief of the love cheat major' by Nick Parker, *The Daily Mail*, 26 February 1992.

Every effort has been made to trace copyright holders in every case. The publishers would be interested to hear from any not acknowledged here.

Guide to Metric Equivalents of English Weights and Measures Mentioned in the Text

Length
1 inch (in) = 2.54 centimetres
1 foot (ft) = 0.3048 metre
1 yard (yd) = 0.9144 metre

Area
1 acre (4840 sq. yd) = 0.405 hectare
1 square inch (sq. in) = 6.4516 square centimetres

Capacity
1 pint (pt) = 0.568 litre

Weight
1 ounce (oz) = 28.35 grammes
1 pound (lb) = 0.454 kilogramme
1 stone (st) = 6.350 kilogrammes

Thermometer scales
Boiling point: 212° Fahrenheit = 100° Centigrade
Freezing point: 32° Fahrenheit = 0° Centigrade